"Minimalism is trending right now, b̶ ▨▨▨▨ ▨▨▨▨ life and embracing simplicity are timeless Christian truths. Hess takes a personalized approach, inviting readers to identify their innate tendencies towards organization and clutter, and to proceed with this personalized knowledge in hand. Equal parts motivational and practical, this book is a gem."

— **Jenny Uebbing**, writer, speaker, and blogger at
Mama Needs Coffee

"I've followed the organizational wisdom of Lisa Lawmaster Hess for years and am thrilled that she has now compiled her wisdom into a single easy-to-implement guide! *Know Thyself* is the one system I've discovered that doesn't try to apply a one-size-fits-all solution, but rather helps me work within my personal tendencies to have a lifestyle, career, and spiritual life that work together to bring satisfaction, productivity and peace. Transform your systems, have fun and see terrific progress working your way through this book!"

— **Lisa M. Hendey**, founder of CatholicMom.com
and author of *I Am God's Storyteller*

"Lisa Hess's book, *Know Thyself*, is an entirely new approach to helping people find a workable solution to organization. It's especially refreshing to read positive and affirming comments throughout. No shaming or blaming permitted in Lisa's world! Her positivity motivates the reader to discover their own step-by-step personalized solution. I highly recommend *Know Thyself* as a must-read."

— **Cindy Bernstein**, professional organizer and
owner of Aim 4 Order, LLC

"Lisa Lawmaster Hess explains how to turn your organizing liabilities into systems that work for you, encouraging you to build on your unique, God-given strengths. In organizing, one size does not fit all; Lisa shows you how to find what fits you best."

— **Barb Szyszkiewicz**, editor at CatholicMom.com and managing editor at *Today's Catholic Teacher*

"*Know Thyself* will change how you think about organizing your life. Lisa Lawmaster Hess's STYLE approach puts strategies in your hands to best determine how, when, and where you organize. Packed with straightforward advice, she will guide you in the right direction."

— **Matthew Randall**, Associate Dean of Career Services at Lebanon Valley College

Know Thyself

KNOW THYSELF

The Imperfectionist's Guide
to Sorting Your Stuff

Lisa Lawmaster Hess

Our Sunday Visitor

www.osv.com
Our Sunday Visitor Publishing Division
Our Sunday Visitor, Inc.
Huntington, Indiana 46750

Our Sunday Visitor Publishing Division
Our Sunday Visitor, Inc.
200 Noll Plaza
Huntington, IN 46750
1-800-348-2440

ISBN: 978-1-68192-323-9 (Inventory No. T1996)
eISBN: 978-1-68192-324-6
LCCN: 2019936406

Cover and interior design: Amanda Falk
Cover and interior art: Shutterstock

PRINTED IN THE UNITED STATES OF AMERICA

To my mom, who would have loved this book and who, given her always immaculate home, could have written one of her own.

Contents

Introduction

*I praise thee, for thou art fearful and
wonderful. Wonderful are thy works!
Thou knowest me right well.*
Psalm 139:14

When it comes to organizing, there are two kinds of people. There are Type A organizers, for whom organizing is easy and automatic. Practical, time-tested tools work for them. They've successfully (and consistently) mastered the use of three-ring binders, file cabinets, and pocket folders. Type A organizers are the embodiment of the phrase "a place for everything and everything in its place."

And then there are the rest of us.

We want to get organized, we really do. Tired of feeling scattered, we buy three-hole punches so we can corral all those loose papers into binders. We buy boxes of multi-colored file folders in an effort to restore order; and we spend hours setting up filing systems only to be stymied by them later and revert to stuffing, cramming, jamming, and putting things in "safe places."

We know that getting organized is a worthwhile goal — a life skill we should cultivate. We understand that we save time and energy when we can find what we need when we need it. We secretly (or not so secretly) envy our put-together, Type A organized friends who make it look so *simple*.

But for us, it's not. In our best moments, we trust that we're smart enough to master this skill, creative enough to cook up new solutions, and fabulous enough to make our homes look stylish in the process. In our moments of weakness, however, we wonder if we somehow got in the wrong line on the day God was handing out organizational skills.

And it makes us feel lousy. And maybe even broken.

But we're *not* broken; we are wonderfully made, and we each organize differently. Traditional tools might not be a good fit for us, but that's a technicality, because organization is more than just the tools we choose. Successful organization requires three components working together:

styles + strategies + tools = organization

Did you notice what came first in that equation? Styles — *your* styles, your very self. God has created each of us to be just the way he wants us to be. If we can tap into the skills and talents he has given us, not only can we organize in a way that's sustainable, but we can also be the best version of ourselves. Instead of trying to mold ourselves to the tools and strategies we think *should* work, we can look for tools and strategies that fit the way we think and the way we organize. We can use our gifts, double-edged swords though they may be, to develop a life skill that saves time and energy and helps us to appreciate how wonderfully made we really are.

When we are organized, we can find what we need when we need it. We have systems that work, and we know where things go. We even develop a sense of peace about our surroundings because we feel in charge of our stuff, not the other way around.

Does all this sound just a little too good to be true? Then, in the spirit of full disclosure, I need to let you know that this is a process — one that takes time and effort. But organization is also more than a process. At its core it's a feeling, one that ebbs and flows as we endeavor to maintain balance between the stuff that comes in and the stuff that goes out. It's possible to look organized without feeling organized (as anyone can attest who's ever tossed stuff into a closet when company's coming), to manage the stuff without creating a system but, when we do, we cheat ourselves. When we feel organized, we worry less about how we look and more about how we function, which is what makes the process worth the time and energy it requires.

You've probably already figured out that the process in this book is a little different from the usual approaches to getting organized. The first step is to look at who you already are and what you already do — the gifts God has given you. Though at first those gifts might look like stumbling blocks, they actually hold the key to getting organized in a way that's true to who you are. Organizing by STYLE (we'll delve into that acronym later) doesn't seek to change your styles but rather to embrace them and to use them as tools to form the foundation of a sustainable system of organization.

Reading this book is the beginning of a journey. Within these pages you'll find tools and strategies that work for your styles so you can relax into a plan that feels like a fit instead of making you want to throw one.

Who knows? It might even be fun.

So, pack your sense of humor, leave all your preconceived notions behind, and join me on the road to organization.

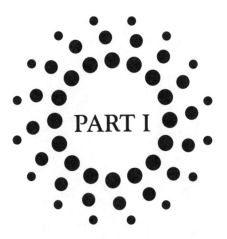

PART I

Identifying Your Personal
and Organizational Styles

CHAPTER 1

You've Got Style!

*To each is given the manifestation of
the Spirit for the common good.*
1 CORINTHIANS 12:7

Saturday morning. The house is quiet, everyone off to his or her own activities. It's time to get this place organized. But how? And where to start?

With no definite plan, but plenty of determination to whip her house into shape, Gemma wanders upstairs and into her seven-year-old son's room. Zane's love for animals is in evidence. Stuffed animals fill fishnet-style hammocks in two corners of his room. More plush companions cover his bed and litter the floor, and his bookshelves are packed with a combination of books, glass animals, plastic animals, clay animals, stuffed animals, and, of course, Zane's dinosaur collection. Scattered among all the animals are the rest of Zane's collections: keychains, erasers, and other assorted treasures, along with a fistful of mulch in a plastic bag smack in the center of his desk. Zane loves stuff.

Gemma closes the door on Zane's collections, hoping her daughter's bedroom will prove to be less of a challenge. Sixteen-year-old Isabelle's bookshelves are lined with novels, and her walls are covered in posters of exotic destinations. A field-hockey stick is propped up in one corner, where it has stood since the season ended four months ago, a reminder that a few minutes of off-season practice might be a good plan. Sketch pads and paint sets are strewn across Isabelle's desk, and a bulletin board above her bed holds half-finished sketches, flute music, and to-do lists. The script for the musical sits propped on her nightstand, with a green highlighter as a book mark. Isabelle needs to see things.

Gemma sighs. Maybe the kids' rooms aren't the best place to start.

Across the hall, the home office Gemma shares with her husband is less chaotic. Evan is a Type A organizer. While a few of Gemma's things are piled on the desk, there's no trace of her husband's belongings anywhere; all his things are neatly filed or put in their place. No wonder he can always seem to find what he needs when he needs it.

Gemma is organized, but in a way that makes sense only to her; and sometimes, even she is baffled by what she was thinking when she put things away. It doesn't help that she's usually stashing things in a rush; between work, church, PTA, and the kids' activities, she never seems to have enough time to keep everything just so. Still, there's no activity Gemma would relinquish. Gemma loves to be busy.

Zane, Isabelle, and Gemma illustrate the three different personal styles we'll discuss in this book: *I love stuff, I love to be busy,* and *I need to see it.* Once we consider each family member's personal styles, it becomes clear that each room has a certain logic.

I love stuff kids like Zane

- develop an attachment to their things;
- are often collectors and sometimes choose unusual things to collect;
- often struggle to part with their things because their "stuff" is important to them; and
- have so much stuff that they often run out of places to put everything.

While the simple solution to a pragmatic, naturally organized person (like Zane's dad, Evan) would be to just get rid of some of the stuff, this is extremely difficult for an *I love stuff* person. And forcing the issue, as Evan has on several occasions, only seems to make Zane more determined to hang on to his precious possessions. Each item, it seems, has a story.

On the other hand, *I need to see it* kids like Isabelle

- leave things out so they'll remember to do them;
- hate to put things away because they fear that out of sight will mean out of mind; and
- replace "to-do" lists with "to-get-to" piles.

What looks like disorganized piles to a Type A organizer is actually a system — sort of — for someone with an *I need to see it* personal style.

And Gemma? She's evidence that these styles don't just apply to kids. *I love to be busy* people like Gemma

- thrive on hectic schedules;
- struggle to manage their things as well as they manage their time; and
- become inundated with stuff because they haven't found or made the time to put things where they belong – if such a place exists.

But personal styles are only half the equation. Now that we've looked at Zane, Isabelle, and Gemma's personal styles, let's look a little further to see if we can uncover their organizational styles.

Gemma decides that she can make quick work of the office, which is less cluttered than the kids' rooms. Gathering up all her folders and piles from the week, she opens one of her desk drawers, but she can't fit everything inside. Setting aside the thickest folder, which has her notes from Bible study, she slides everything else into the drawer, then looks around the room for somewhere to put the final folder. A glance at the open closet reveals space on one of the shelves, so she hastily stashes the folder there, closes the door, and surveys the space. One room down. Gemma's organizational style? *I know I put it somewhere*.

Back in Zane's room, Gemma must admit that the room looks better than it did earlier in the week. Zane had invited a friend over, and desperate to find two specific toys, he'd torn his room apart, dumping the animal hammocks and digging through containers. By the time he'd remembered that Gemma had given him a plastic container to put them in the last time they'd cleaned the room, the floor was littered with animals. When Gemma saw Zane's room, she laid down the law: no play date until the room was put back together. Not wanting to turn away his friend, Zane quickly stuffed the animals back into their hammocks and shoved everything else into drawers and under his bed. Zane's organizational style is *cram and jam.*

That same evening, Isabelle wanted to finish sketches she'd started several months earlier; she hoped the director might consider them as part of the set for the musical. Isabelle checked the sketches on her bulletin board but found only one of the drawings. She pulled it down and repinned the rest of the sketches back onto the bulletin board before attacking the piles on her desk. Pushing aside a pile of half-read books, Isabelle uncovered her sketchbook, but the drawings she wanted weren't inside. Frustrated, she took her mother's advice to retrace her steps. Picking up her book bag from the middle of the floor where she'd dropped it earlier in the day, Isabelle pulled out folders, notebooks, journals, and books. When she found the sketches tucked into a folder with her rehearsal schedule, she remembered that she'd taken them with her to rehearsal. Leaving her open backpack on the floor with its contents scattered beside it, Isabelle sat down at her desk to work on her sketches. Isabelle's organizational style is *drop and run.*

Despite their struggles, Zane, Isabelle, and Gemma are more organized than they seem. They simply need to learn to use their default actions (dropping and running, for example) as clues, and transform them into organizational concepts they can use consistently. As with the personal styles, the first step is to identify the style that's at work and look at the traits that go with it.

I know I put it somewhere people like Gemma

- may look organized, but struggle to find what they need when they need it;
- are likely to have a wide variety of unrelated things stashed together;
- organize by putting things in the place that is

most convenient at the moment, rather than in a logical place; and
- lack a system and/or fail to establish consistent homes for their belongings.

Cram and jam kids like Zane

- cram things into any available open space, and jam things into spaces that are already overcrowded;
- lack an understanding of the concept of "full";
- rarely have an organizational system, unless it's for things that are extremely important to them; and
- may look organized — until you open up the closets and look inside the drawers.

Drop and run kids like Isabelle

- put things down instead of away;
- are unlikely to utilize systems that require multiple steps;
- can often find things where they last used them; and
- often need to retrace their steps to locate misplaced items.

Do any of the descriptions sound familiar? Take a look at the chart below and decide where you think you fit, choosing one description from the top row and one from the bottom row. Then, take the quiz on the next page to see if you can narrow things down.

I love stuff	I love to be busy	I love to see it
WHAT'S YOUR STYLE?		
I know I put it somewhere	Cram and Jam	Drop and run

Personal and Organizational Styles Quiz

Mark each item below as true or false.

1. You participate in so many activities that you have something to do nearly every night. **T** **F**

2. The only way you remember to bring things with you when you leave the house is to leave them out where you're likely to trip over them. **T** **F**

3. At least one closet, dresser, or other space in your home has a number of items you no longer really need but can't seem to get rid of. **T** **F**

4. Your house looks neat, yet you struggle to find what you need when you need it. **T** **F**

5. No matter how neat your papers are when you put them away, they always seem to end up wrinkled and/or torn. **T** **F**

6. One look at your workspace, bed, counter, or floor reveals evidence of everything you've done in the last few days. T F

7. Though you've tried, you rarely manage to put papers in the rings of three-ring binders or the pockets of pocket folders. T F

8. You can often find lost items by retracing your steps. T F

9. You often feel bored when you have unscheduled time. T F

10. You have more stuff than room to store it. T F

11. You put things away, but often forget which "safe place" you put them in. T F

12. You often forget things if you don't write them down. T F

All finished? Now let's compare your answers on the quiz to the key below. Every "true" is a clue:

1. I love to be busy.
2. I need to see it.
3. I love stuff.
4. I know I put it somewhere.
5. Cram and jam.
6. Drop and run.
7. Cram and jam or I need to see it.
8. Drop and run.
9. I love to be busy.
10. I love stuff.

11. I know I put it somewhere.
12. I need to see it.

Do the quiz answers match your predictions and observations? For most people, clear patterns will emerge, and the answers will come as no surprise. What they've noticed about the way they organize (or don't) will match what they've predicted and where their answers land on the quiz.

Some people will be "a little bit of this and a little bit of that." At this point in the process, that's to be expected. Further observation, discussion, and exploration will help you determine your predominant styles. And some people really are a mix of styles, which can be beneficial. An overlap means more strategies to work with!

The most important thing to keep in mind right now is that there are no right or wrong answers on the quiz, and these styles are not personal or organizational flaws.

This shift in thinking can be challenging. Up to this point, these styles have probably been stumbling blocks to your organizational efforts, perhaps even traits you found embarrassing. Moving forward, the goal will not be to change your styles, but rather to help you view your natural tendencies as assets rather than liabilities.

But Organizing by STYLE is more than just relabeling habits. When we accept our styles as manifestations of our personalities and our natural tendencies, we can look at them in a different light. This change in perspective frees up the energy we've wasted beating ourselves up and allows us to expend it instead on finding practical solutions to our organizational struggles. By discovering the benefits inherent in our styles, we can use who we are and what we do automatically as a blueprint for developing a workable, sustainable plan. Best of all, since the basis of this plan is no longer who someone else thinks we should be or what someone else thinks we should do, we're better able to celebrate exactly who God created us to be — organizational challenges and all. We might even find a little time to give thanks for the traits we once grumbled about.

Could you work to change your styles? Of course. But if you're reading this book, I suspect you've already tried that approach, only to land back where you began. Besides, isn't working with yourself a whole lot easier than working against yourself?

Part I of this book will focus on helping you to pinpoint your styles. There will be no judgment, no shaming, and no attempt to convert you to another, "better" way of doing things. (The world has plenty of traditionally organized Type A organizers like Evan.) I hope that this book will help you to uncover the unique manifestations of the Spirit that God has given you and help you figure out how to use them as your guide. The goal is not perfection, but rather a system that makes it easy for you to find what you need when you need it.

In part II, we'll play with some strategies to go with your styles. Each chapter will focus on one letter of the STYLE acronym:

> **S**tart with successes
> **T**ake small steps
> **Y**es, it has a home!
> **L**et it go
> **E**asy upkeep

Finally, in part III, we'll extend the basics and conclude with some shortcuts and reminders to give you a boost when time is short and you need a quick refresher.

Please note my choice of pronoun: "we." I am an *I need to see it/drop and run* girl, and will be until the day I die. Make no mistake — I'm on this journey with you.

Let's get started.

CHAPTER 2

Personal Styles:
How We're Wired

*Now there are varieties of gifts, but the
same Spirit; and there are varieties of
service, but the same Lord.*
1 CORINTHIANS 12:4-5

In chapter 1, we identified Gemma as *I love to be busy/drop and run*. *I love to be busy* is Gemma's personal style. Personal styles, an integral part of who we are, influence the way we organize. The three personal styles are *I love stuff*, *I love to be busy*, and *I need to see it*. When you took the quiz in chapter 1, which personal style described you? Feel free to skip ahead and read that section of this chapter first if you wish. Then, double back and look over the information about the other styles to see if you can pick up a few additional ideas. Although each of the styles can pose challenges when it comes to organization, all three can be pressed into service in a positive fashion.

I LOVE STUFF

What it looks like: Like Zane in chapter 1, those with an *I love stuff* personal style are collectors, with an eye for unusual treasures. As a result, they become very attached to their things, which makes culling collections and — gasp! — getting rid of things very difficult. This can create a space issue, as those with an *I love stuff* personal style often accumulate more things than they have room for.

The heart of the problem: too much stuff, not enough space.

Positive attributes: An attraction to unique items that, when applied to containers and other storage tools, can add a flair to organizational systems and beauty to their surroundings. Their affinity for collecting often makes those with the *I love stuff* personal style very good at creating unusual and eye-catching combinations of items. In addition, those with an *I love stuff* personal style are often very good at finding creative uses for everyday things.

Putting it to work: The skill of keeping like items together often comes naturally to those with an *I love stuff* personal style. This is key to organization, since a cluster of similar items or treasures united by a theme looks neater than a haphazard group of items that appears to have been dumped on a shelf or table. Unrelated items look like clutter. Items that go together look like a collection. This "like items together" mentality also gives those with an *I love stuff* personal style an edge when it comes to finding logical homes for their things.

Organizational systems rooted in the *I love stuff* style pair beauty and function. Look for ways to make your "stuff" do double duty, such as storing keys inside a pretty pottery dish or using colorful baskets for storage. When acquiring new pieces, plan ahead. Is this item decorative? functional? both? Can you imagine where it will fit in your home? Use the answers to these questions to make deliberate decisions about what comes home with you and what you're satisfied to admire from afar.

When it comes to collections, set aside a special spot for displaying those that are more decorative than functional. If your collections overwhelm your space, try rotating them, one collection per room or season, so that each gets time in the spotlight.

The process of rotating collections can also reveal which items are the most beloved. Examine your feelings when it's time to take the collection-in-waiting out for display. Are you excited to do this, or could you just as easily leave it out of sight? If it's the latter, consider finding a new home (outside your home) for that particular collection, or at least part of it. As part of this process, also examine the items in each collection as you move it from displayed to undisplayed and back again. Is every piece still something you want to keep? If so, then do so. If not, consider downsizing the collection by donating or selling pieces you've grown tired of. We'll talk more about nontraumatic ways of letting things go in chapter 7.

I LOVE TO BE BUSY

What it looks like: Those with an *I love to be busy* personal style get things done. As with Gemma in chapter 1, this generosity of spirit can sometimes lead to overbooking, which may leave those with this personal style feeling overwhelmed or stressed, leading to pileups. As those with this style run from one place to another, they may lack the time and energy to put each activity's stuff where it belongs — if they've even designated a space for it — let alone keep up with the influx of new things.

The heart of the problem: too much to do, not enough time.

Positive attributes: In addition to being generous with their time, folks with an *I love to be busy* personal style are usually excellent time managers. Because the things they commit to are things they genuinely love and/or want to do, *I love to be busy* people manage to squeeze a lot of activity into a little bit of time. The skills of sticking to a schedule, managing small blocks of time, and categorizing — all of which are strong suits for those with an *I love to be busy* personal style — are important tools when it comes to organizing not just time, but things as well.

Putting it to work: Those with an *I love to be busy* personal style often benefit from putting their categorizing skills to work by creating separate storage, preferably of the grab-and-go variety, for each activity. Catechist materials go in one tote bag, book club materials in another, knitting in a third, and so on, with each bag or container being replenished right after it's been used. The trick is to put those superior scheduling skills to work as well, building in time to take everything out, remove any time sensitive information, sharpen pencils, replenish supplies, and put everything back into the bag so it's ready to grab and go the next time it's needed. Ideally, each container should be well-suited to its purpose so that all necessary supplies have specific homes within the container or bag. This makes a quick once-over easier on those days when the replenishment of the bag just didn't happen. Scheduling time to keep up with the flow of stuff is especially important for those whose schedules are packed. Luckily, scheduling comes naturally for most people with an *I love to be busy* personal style.

No matter their storage preferences, those with an *I love to be busy* personal style will need to establish consistent homes for their things, particularly those they need to grab quickly on their way out the door. We'll talk more about homes and locations in chapter 6.

One essential tool for those with an *I love to be busy* personal style is a calendar or planner. For some, a single calendar for everything makes sense; for others, a combination approach works better. The specifics of the planner — whether it's electronic, paper and pencil, a bullet journal, or a white board on the refrigerator color-coded by activity — matters less than its ease of use. If you're getting where you need to be on time on a regular basis, without missed appointments and forgotten commitments, your planner system is probably a good one.

I NEED TO SEE IT

What it looks like: Just like the other two personal styles, the *I need to see it* personal style is just what it sounds like. Afraid that out of sight will mean out of mind, those with this personal style leave physical reminders for every important task out in plain sight. While leaving a backpack and lunch bag beside the door isn't such a big deal, the *I need to see it* reminder plan can become problematic if those with this style have lots of interests (like Isabelle in chapter 1), have lots of things to remember, and/or fail to put away these physical reminders once the task has been completed.

The heart of the problem: attempting to use piles as a workable organizational system.

Positive attributes: optimism and categorizing. Those with an *I need to see it* personal style really do believe they're going to be able to do all those things in all those piles — and some days, they do. And because their piles are their system, just one pile won't do. Each pile represents a category or line item on a list. Tossing everything into one stack might look neater, but a single pile often defeats the purpose for those with this personal style.

Putting it to work: Keeping things visible is the key to success for those with this personal style. Containers and folders that are clear, color-coded, or labeled will beat out traditional tools such as binders, pocket folders, and file cabinets every time. Shelves work better than drawers, but subdividing drawers also works well; when a single glance reveals everything inside the open drawer, it's less intimidating to put things in the drawer (out of sight) in the first place. File boxes with open tops also work well, especially when combined with colored file folders. The more see-through, colorful, patterned, or unique the storage, the better. The goal is to maintain the visual nudge by using something neater and more organized than piles.

So why not just make lists? If you have to ask that, you don't have an *I need to see it* personal style. *I need to see it* folks do make lists; we just supplement them with piles. Items on a list blend together into a unified whole, causing individual items to disappear onto the page; crossing items off a list, no matter how motivating, can't top reducing and removing piles from a horizontal surface. When the piles are gone, the *I need to see it* person knows she's finished. Unfortunately, the piles are rarely gone.

CAN I HAVE MORE THAN ONE STYLE?

When I first share the styles quiz, I frequently get the question, "Can I be all of them?" The answer is yes ... and no.

While it's possible to have elements of each of the styles, most of us end up identifying one predominant personal style and one predominant organizational style. These styles pave the way to organizational systems that play to our strengths. But even though our predominant styles form the foundation of our organizational systems, the traits we share with other styles broaden the range of tools that work for us. Combining the tool options that work for our primary styles with those that work from other styles allows us more choices and helps us to infuse creativity into our organizational plans.

For example, even though my predominant personal style is *I need to see it*, I can also identify with both of the other personal styles, *I love stuff* and *I love to be busy*. Because of this, I can adopt tools and strategies from these styles, as long as they work with my primary style. No matter how pretty, cool, or unique the container, if it doesn't give me the visual nudge I need, it will be an obstacle rather than a tool.

Confused? Here's the simple version. Use your primary styles — one personal style and one organizational style — as the foundation of your organizational system. Then use your tendencies from the other styles to build on that foundation, adding variety and creativity while staying true to what works.

Oh — and don't forget to have fun.

Smart organizers know when to ask for help

Dear Lord, help me to remember that my personal styles are a part of the me you created. Help me to use them in constructive ways so that I may be more at peace with myself and with all that surrounds me. Amen.

Chomping at the bit to get started, even though we're only in chapter 2? Go for it! Check out this chart on containers by personal style. A "yes" means that type of container is a good match for the style; a "no" means just the opposite. Blank cells are "maybes" — containers that fall somewhere in between and are more a matter of personal preference.

	I love stuff	I love to be busy	I need to see it
Clear			YES
Lidded			
All one color			NO
Color-coded		YES	
Labeled		YES	YES
Unusual or unique	YES		YES
Flexible (e.g., fabric)			
Divided or sectioned	YES	YES	YES
Open	YES		

LISA'S LISTS
Three Things to Remember

1. **Every style has positive attributes.** Because our styles have most likely gotten in our way in the past, it's easy to see them only as stumbling blocks. But once we acknowledge and embrace our styles, we can use them to our advantage. When we adopt this new perspective, we unlock the potential behind our styles as tools for getting organized in a way that makes sense to us and is therefore sustainable.

2. **A sense of humor is an important tool in the organizing arsenal.** Because you're reading this book, I'm assuming you have a sense of humor, but it's been subjugated by the judgments you (and perhaps others) have made about the very styles I'm asking you to embrace. Why not try dusting off that sense of humor and taking a more lighthearted approach? At the very least, it'll save you from expending energy on making yourself feel bad, and at best it can lead you to a self-acceptance that enables you to come up with creative ways of using your styles in ways that work for you. Either way, you'll have smiled.

3. **It's a process.** Identifying your personal and organizational styles is the first step in this one-step-forward-two-steps-back process. Some days you'll feel like an organizational guru and other days, you'll feel like the Queen (or King) of Chaos. Baby steps.

CHAPTER 3

Organizational Styles: Our Default Settings

And there are varieties of working, but it is the same God who inspires them all in every one.
1 CORINTHIANS 12:6

If the personal styles are the "who" behind our organizational systems, the organizational styles are the "how" — our organizational defaults, as it were. In this chapter, we'll explore the organizational styles — *I know I put it somewhere, cram and jam,* and *drop and run* — just as we did with the personal styles in chapter 2. Once again, feel free to skip ahead to the section of this chapter that matches your style and then come back to the information about the other styles to see if you can pick up any additional hints.

Let's start with the organizational style we identified for Gemma in chapter 1: *I know I put it somewhere.*

I KNOW I PUT IT SOMEWHERE

What it looks like: Those with an *I know I put it somewhere* organizational style typically look organized. Desktops and tabletops are usually clear, piles are safely put away, and everything looks neat and tidy. The problem? Those with this style aren't consistent or systematic. They like things to look nice, so they stash things wherever there's room. Then, when it comes time to retrieve what they need, they can't remember where they put it.

The heart of the problem: lack of a consistent, cohesive system.

Positive attributes: Folks with an *I know I put it somewhere* organizational style are good at putting things away. They find a place for everything, even if the places they find are inconsistent or illogical. They have the basics of storage down; they just need a little guidance to bring their retrieval skills up to the same level.

Putting it to work: Those with an *I know I put it somewhere* organizational style need a system. By establishing consistent homes for their things in logical locations, folks with this organizational style can shape their natural tendency to put things away into a system that also enables them to find what they need when they need it. What kinds of tools work for those with an *I know I put it somewhere* organizational style? The kinds that create built-in reminders. Clear containers, divided containers, and open storage keep things visible, while labeled locations and unique, unusual or eye-catching organizers provide a hint as to what's inside. *I know I put it somewhere* organizers might also benefit from a small location notebook where they keep track of locations for infrequently used items such as holiday decorations or gifts. Sound silly? When is the last time you said to yourself, "Oh, I'll remember I put this here," and then didn't?

CRAM AND JAM

What it looks like: Those with a *cram and jam* organizational style don't waste any space. Instead, they do just what the style says — they cram things into nooks, and they jam things into crannies. Sometimes everything gets crammed and jammed into the same space (think backpacks and drawers); other times, the *cram and jammer* finds crevices no one else would consider storage and stuffs things there. Consequently, the things they've stored might not be in great shape upon retrieval; in fact, they are often rumpled, crumpled, and/or broken.

The heart of the problem: overstuffing.

Positive attributes: Those with the *cram and jam* organizational style are efficient in their use of space. In addition, when those with this organizational style consistently use the same spaces, they have little trouble finding what they need when they need it. It may take some digging, but *cram and jammers* can usually excavate what they need.

Putting it to work: Folks with the *cram and jam* organizational style often do better with open storage than enclosed spaces: shelves instead of drawers, for example. Many *cram and jam*mers have already mastered the art of consistently putting things in the same spot, so the trick is to give them space in which to work. Soft, expandable containers (fabric bins, for example) can work better to keep things in good condition than rigid materials like wood and plastic, as can containers with room to grow. The tighter the space, the more likely the items going into it will come out wrinkled or damaged.

DROP AND RUN

What it looks like: Those with a *drop and run* organizational style leave a trail in their wake. They walk in the door, take off their shoes (and leave them by the door), drop whatever they're carrying, and go on to the next thing they want to do. If they happen to need something they brought into the house, they'll take it with them. Otherwise, the bag, backpack, coat, or other paraphernalia is likely to stay wherever they dropped it.

The heart of the problem: putting it down instead of putting it away.

Positive attributes: organizational sonar. Those with the *drop and run* organizational style are amazing step retracers. They can extract an item from a pile based on its location, which tells them when they last used the thing they're looking for.

Putting it to work: Make it as easy to put things away as it is to put them down. One-step storage systems, containers, hooks, pegboards located where the *drop and run* organizer is likely to drop things before running, unlidded containers — all these provide ready storage solutions to help shape the *drop and run* tendency into an organizational habit that works. Choosing key locations for these containers helps the *drop and run* organizer transition from dropping things wherever to dropping them where they belong.

• • •

Did you notice one piece of advice reappearing across the styles? No matter your organizational style, establishing consistent homes for things — especially those you use often — is the biggest time-saver you can add to your organizational toolbox. While the containers we choose will be unique to our styles, putting the same item in the same place every time saves time. Because we know exactly where to find it, we don't waste time looking for it.

Now that we've fleshed out the personal and organizational styles, take a minute to consider where you've landed. If you had to choose *one* primary personal style (*I love stuff, I love to be busy,* or *I need to see it*) and *one* primary organizational style (*I know I put it somewhere, cram and jam,* or *drop and run*), which would you choose? Use the worksheet and containers chart on the following pages to flesh out your ideas and begin to think about how your personal and organizational styles can work together.

Smart organizers know when to ask for help

Dear Lord, help me to remember that my organizational styles are a part of the me you created. Give me the wisdom to expend my energy on finding the good in who I am, rather than wasting it on judgments that keep me from appreciating what I have to offer. Amen.

Style Sheets

Personal Styles

My *primary* personal style is:

But I also identify with the personal style:

Because:

The *best* part of my primary personal style is:

The part of my primary personal style that's most challenging is:

Organizational Styles

My primary organizational style is:

But I also identify with the organizational style:

Because:

The best part of my primary organizational style is:

The part of my primary organizational style that's most challenging is:

Containers and Systems

When I look at the chart on the next page, the containers I find most appealing are:

There is/isn't crossover between the suggested containers for my primary personal style and the suggested containers for my primary organizational style.

Remember this chart from chapter 2? Now we've added the organizational styles. A "yes" means that type of container is a good match for the style; a "no" means just the opposite. Blank cells are "maybes" — containers that fall somewhere in between and are more a matter of personal preference. This time, as you scan the chart, go down the columns, and look for containers that are a yes or a maybe for both your personal style and your organizational style.

	I love stuff	I love to be busy	I need to see it	I know I put it some-where	Cram & jam	Drop & run
Clear			YES	YES	YES	YES
Lidded				NO	NO	
All one color			NO	NO		
Color-coded		YES		YES		YES
Labeled		YES	YES	YES		YES
Unusual or unique	YES		YES	YES		YES
Flexible (e.g., fabric)					YES	
Divided or sectioned	YES	YES	YES			
Open	YES				YES	YES

LISA'S LISTS
Three More Things to Remember

1. **Every style has attributes.** This is true for organizational styles just as it is for personal styles. Although the organizational styles described in this chapter fly in the face of traditional methods, each still has an element of organizational logic behind it. Working with our styles makes organizing less of a hassle, and choosing tools that make sense based on what we do naturally makes it more likely that we'll use them on a consistent and long-term basis.

2. **We organize best when we integrate our personal and organizational styles.** Sound difficult? It's not. Because both our personal and organizational styles are what we do naturally, we've already integrated them within ourselves. The next step is choosing the tools that work for both of our styles and purposefully using them in ways that work for us.

3. **There is no one right answer.** Two people could have the same personal and organizational styles but choose completely different ways of putting them to work. Style and taste preferences, available space, and a multitude of other factors will determine what shape each person's organizational system takes.

PART II

Organizing by STYLE

CHAPTER 4

S: Start with Successes

Having gifts that differ according to the
grace given to us, let us use them.
ROMANS 12:6

In part I, we identified and described personal and organizational styles and how they fit together, and took a brief look at some of the basic strategies that work for each of them. In part II, we'll take a look at a different kind of STYLE: the process we'll use to take ourselves from where we are to where we want to be. Each chapter in part II will focus on one letter of the STYLE acronym:

Start with successes
Take small steps
Yes, it has a home!
Let it go
Easy upkeep

In addition to being part of a process, each step stands alone and is a strategy we can return to as we troubleshoot problem areas or systems that aren't quite working. Keep in mind that these steps should work for you, not the other way around. They are prompts, not hard-and-fast rules, meant to remind you of your organizational goals.

Ready to dig in? Let's move from theory to practice. Grab your Style Sheets from chapter 3 and choose a starting point. It can be as small as a closet or as big as a bedroom. It can be the space you're proudest of, or it can be the space most in need of improvement.

At my house, if I wanted to start with a place that's in good shape, I'd go stand in my living room. If I wanted a challenge, I'd stand in the doorway of my too-small, not-enough-storage home office or beside my dining room table, which tends to be a magnet for all things paper. Regardless of which space I choose, I will find organizational successes and, most likely, organizational challenges.

And that's the purpose of this task.

So, there you are, standing in (or outside of) the space you've chosen. Glance down at your Style Sheets and remind yourself of the best part of your primary style. Then, take in the space as impartially as possible. What organizational successes can you find? Let's use my office as an example because it contains both successes and challenges. Under the counter, I have labeled decorative boxes containing information for the classes I teach. The boxes match, which makes them look nice, but also makes the labels essential so I can tell what's inside. My personal style is *I need to see it*, which means that unlabeled matching boxes would be an organizational nightmare. The labels, which are handwritten on 1 1/2" x 2" sticky notes (sticky enough to stay put, easy enough to remove if I change my mind), allow me to see at a glance what's inside each box. In addition, those labels nudge me to put course material for only one particular topic inside each box. Looking closely, I see that I got lazy and stuck some papers on top of one of the boxes instead of inside of it, a piece of information we'll come back to later. For now, what's important is that the matched boxes, usually a no-no for someone like me with an *I need to see it* personal style, work because they are labeled, because their pattern is distinct and attractive (a key element to containers for many of the styles), and because I have limited the contents of each box to one very specific type of material. These boxes are one of my successes.

Above the counter, I have two cabinets (kitchen cabinets selected specifically for this space, even though it's not a kitchen). When I open the doors, I can see everything they hold. Nothing is tossed in haphazardly or in random piles. Bins that hold supplies are labeled. With one glance, I can see everything inside the cupboards. These cabinets, too, are a success.

If I were to evaluate the room completely, I could find more successes, as well as numerous things that are not working so well at the moment (like those papers I stuck on top of the boxes instead of inside them). But, for this initial assessment, we are setting the challenges aside — we'll deal with those in a bit.

Take a moment to look at the space you've chosen as impartially as possible, paying special attention to areas, no matter how small, that are organized. Then, answer these three questions:

- Where are my successes?
- What makes them successes?
- How do they connect with my styles?

Go ahead. I'll wait right here.

• • •

What did your assessment reveal? Can you find any patterns? A particular system, container, or routine that keeps part of this space in order?

Your successes are the foundation of your organizational system. If something is working here, chances are you can make that same something (or something like it) work in other areas of your house as well. It doesn't matter if the tools you're using aren't designed to work in other spaces; the only design rules that matter are the ones that contribute to a system that works for you. My home office has a kitchen countertop and kitchen cabinets because that was what worked *with* the space and *for* my styles. And those boxes I pressed into service for course materials? Pressboard gift boxes purchased at half price after Christmas. Not what they were made to do either. But they work, *and* they look nice. Win-win.

Since Organizing by STYLE is nothing if not practical, we're going to take a moment to look at the flip side too. But before I set you loose to look at what's not working, I'm setting some parameters about the answers you're allowed to give to the "why it's not working" question. You may not answer that question with "because I'm lazy/stupid/hopelessly disorganized" or any similar response. In addition to being personally hurtful (and wrong), those answers are organizational dead ends. They say that you're flawed and that's the end of the story.

Well, we're all flawed. But that's not the end of the story.

If you can analyze why part of a system isn't working, you can eliminate every other system that operates the same way from your arsenal of organizing tools. That streamlines your choices, helping you to focus on what might work instead.

Let's go back to my boxes full of course materials, zooming in on the one on the top right in particular, where I stacked the papers on top instead of putting them inside. I know exactly why I did that. The short/nonacceptable answer: because I'm lazy.

See how useful that wasn't?

Let's dig a little deeper. "Lazy" is code for "the system is too complicated for me to use it consistently." I just said I loved my boxes (and I do!) because they're eye-catching and easy to use. After all, what's so hard about lifting a lid and sticking papers inside?

Inside this particular box are not one but two pocket folders (anathema to many styles, including my primary organizational style, which is *drop and run*). Since I couldn't just *drop and run*, I took a shortcut, saving the work for later, when I'd have time to file them properly.

So, now that I know why the system broke down, what do I do? Here are three possibilities:

- I can keep my system as is because it works most of the time.
- I can replace the pocket folders with something more style-friendly.
- I can add another box to the system so I can eliminate the need for the folders inside.

Since I really like the system from both an organizational and a visual perspective, I don't want to overhaul the whole thing. If I had room for another box, I'd go with that option; this problem arose because I have one box that no longer has room to grow. But since I'm pressed for space, that's not an option. Perhaps, in this case, my full-to-capacity box is an indication that it's time to weed out its contents.

Once I've done this, I still have another choice to consider: replace the color-coded pocket folders (one for each class) with colored file folders, no pockets. Previous experience tells me that this will work just fine. But what if it doesn't? Easy. I trouble-shoot again.

How often do you need to troubleshoot? Until you find the solution that works for you.

Okay, your turn. Take a moment and look at the space again. As you jot down the things that don't work for you, remember that recriminations are not helpful, but observations are. Also, keep in mind that "tidy" and "organized" are not the same things. A clear desktop may be tidy, but the desk itself is organized only if the drawers aren't stuffed haphazardly with things that would otherwise be on top of the desk. As you troubleshoot, consider the following:

- What's not working? How can you tell?
- Why isn't it working? (Remember to identify what's wrong with the system.)
- Is the problem a style mismatch?

Go ahead. I'll wait right here.

• • •

What did your assessment reveal? Can you find any patterns? A particular system, container, or routine that's standing between you and an organized space?

Now for the bonus question: Can you replace something that's not working with something that is?

Yes you can. Locate your organizational style in the second set of Style Sheets that begin on the next page. Use your observations to fill in the missing sections (yes, you can write in this book!) and circle or highlight the suggestions that ring true for you. Then do the same with your personal styles.

Putting Your Organizational Styles to Work

If your organizational style is
I know I put it somewhere

Focus on establishing consistent homes for everything and putting things away a little at time.

Tools of choice: clear or labeled containers.

You might also like containers that are distinctive or unique.

With this style, I am successful when:

Some things that don't work for me are:

If your organizational style is
cram and jam

Focus on establishing consistent homes for everything and making sure containers are the right size plus wiggle room.

Tools of choice: open containers and one-step organizational systems.

You might also like containers that are wide enough (and flexible enough) to accommodate stuffing without damage.

With this style, I am successful when:

Some things that don't work for me are:

If your organizational style is
drop and run

Focus on establishing consistent homes for everything and putting one thing away before starting another.

Tools of choice: labeled containers and simple, one-step organizational systems.

You might also like containers that make it as easy to put things away as it is to leave them out.

With this style, I am successful when:

Some things that don't work for me are:

Putting Your Personal Styles to Work

If your personal style is
I love stuff

Focus on keeping only things you love and finding special homes for them, whether out on display or tucked away in consistent locations.

Tools of choice: containers in a variety of sizes, and divided containers for collections.

You might also like containers that show off items of special importance.

With this style, I am successful when:

Some things that don't work for me are:

If your personal style is
I love to be busy

Focus on organizational systems that require little time to maintain.

Tools of choice: one-step organizational systems; separate storage for each activity; compartmentalized containers so you can quickly see what's missing.

You might also like separate containers for each activity.

With this style, I am successful when:

Some things that don't work for me are:

If your personal style is
I need to see it

Focus on keeping things visible and using lists instead of piles, where possible.

Tools of choice: clear, color-coded, or labeled containers; no lids.

You might also like containers that are attractive, unique, or reflect your personality.

With this style, I am successful when:

Some things that don't work for me are:

•••

Take a look at what you've written. This is your blueprint, your foundation. From here on out, the goal is to use more of what works and less of what doesn't. This is simultaneously simple (use what works) and overwhelming (find replacements for what doesn't) because it involves not only building on our strengths but also breaking old habits.

Take a second look at one area that's not working. How long have you been trying to make it work? If you'd found a better solution, you'd have implemented it, right?

Only if you'd known there was a better solution in the first place.

That's what the Style Sheets are all about. The more you dissect what you've been doing, the more ideas you'll get and the more focused you'll be as you move forward. Once we know what works and what doesn't, decisions become easier. We no longer waste money buying things that "should" work, or time trying to fit our styles into a system that doesn't fit.

If you wish, you can expand this exercise to more areas in the living space of your home, or, alternatively, to your work-place, your vehicle, or any other spot you want to organize. As you do so, keep adding to your Style Sheets to create a blue-print you can use as we move into chapter 5 and begin taking small steps.

If you feel yourself getting overwhelmed or losing confi-dence, stop and take a break. Doing so isn't weakness, but rather a part of the process. It takes time to absorb all the new information you're reading and discovering. If you let the ideas simmer, so to speak, they'll begin to gel, so that when you tackle each of the spaces on your list, you'll immediately know what needs to go, and perhaps have almost as certain an idea of what needs to stay.

When we stop looking for perfection, it's easy to spot organi-zational successes. These successes matter. They remind us that we know what we're doing, no matter how lived-in or imperfect our homes and organizational systems may be. When we focus more on what we're doing well than what we're doing wrong, not only do we feel better, but we learn what to replicate in other areas and what to strive for to take spaces in our homes from cluttered to clear.

Even better, when we pair this with our styles, we find the tools we need to determine strategies to take us from frustration to organization.

STRATEGIES FOR THE STYLES

What can you add to your style sheet? Pencil in any of the discoveries below that apply (even if they're listed with a style besides yours) and write in any others you encountered.

Personal Styles

I love stuff: Did you discover like items stored or displayed together? Congratulations! This is a key storage concept and a topic we'll discuss in chapter 6.

I love to be busy: Do you have a planner, calendar, or other time-management tool that's working? Congratulations! This is a key concept for successful time management (more on that in chapter 11), essential to those with an *I love to be busy* personal style.

I need to see it: Did you discover a container or storage system that works for you because of its visual appeal? Congratulations! This is a key organizational concept for those with the *I need to see it* personal style. More on that in chapter 6.

Organizational Styles

I know I put it somewhere: Did you find a stash of things all safely stored in the same place? Congratulations! This is a key storage concept and a topic we'll discuss in chapter 6.

Cram and jam: Did you find one container or storage space that allows you to use the "everything in one place" philosophy well and without damage to the things stored there? Congratulations! Finding tools that work with your styles is foundational to an organizational system that works. We'll talk more about this in chapter 6.

Drop and run: Did you find some things that were consistently put away, or a container that made it easy to put things where they belong instead of where it's most convenient to drop them? Congratulations! Finding the tools that make it as easy to put things away as it is to simply put them down is foundational to an organizational system that works. We'll talk more about this in chapter 6.

• • •

Now, take a look at your Style Sheets. Do you see things you're doing right? Congratulate yourself.

Things that need to be changed? We'll work on that.

Can you see patterns among the things that work and those that don't? You're on your way. Let's take some small steps forward.

KNOW THYSELF

I love giving compliments — even to complete strangers — but I'm terrible at receiving them. I'm not embarrassed by them, nor am I afraid to acknowledge that I have actual talents, but somehow I can't seem to simply say "thank you." I need to explain, expand, or brush off the kind words. Sometimes I'm afraid I make others sorry they said anything in the first place.

God didn't give us gifts so we could hide (or explain) them away. He gave them to us so we could use them. In acknowledging our gifts and sharing them with those around us, we give him glory because those gifts are ours through him.

Do you know what you're good at? Or are you afraid that acknowledging your gifts makes you sound conceited? As you search for your organizational successes, consider it an exercise in gratitude. Every time you discover a talent, say a prayer of thanks to the God who blessed you with it. And then put it to use to honor him.

Smart organizers know when to ask for help

Dear Lord, thank you for helping me to recognize the good you have placed in me. Help me to embrace my uniqueness and take time to appreciate the things I do well. Help me to recognize my strengths as gifts from you and trust that those gifts will, with your help, give me the tools I need to overcome the things I find challenging. Amen.

LISA'S LISTS

Success Scavenger Hunt

Every home, office, vehicle, and other space has areas that are working. How many of these can you find in the space you're STYLE-ing?

1. **One spot that is organized to your satisfaction.** A counter? A closet? A drawer? Something else? Once you find it, analyze it. Why is it working?

2. **One container that you absolutely love.** What do you love about it? The look? The use? The size? Is it earning its keep, or would it be more helpful to you somewhere else?

3. **One spot that's *almost* there organizationally.** Organization is an imperfect art. Often, we move incrementally closer to the solutions we're seeking. When we stop focusing on what's wrong and consider what's right, the final baby step to the solution often presents itself. What would take this spot from almost to organized?

4. **One container that you absolutely hate.** How is this a success? Easy. Organizing by STYLE requires us to determine what works and what doesn't so that we replicate the former not the latter. If you can identify what's not working and why it's not working, you can avoid falling into the same organizational (or aesthetic) trap as you move forward. What's one tool you'll stop trying to force yourself to use?

5. **One surface that's entirely clear.** For those who struggle with organization, clear surfaces can be hard to come by and are worth celebrating. Why is this one clear when others are not? Is the plan for keeping this surface clear one you can use elsewhere?

6. **One spot that's working for someone else, but not for you.** If you share space with other people, you're bound to find style differences. What makes that spot workable for someone else, but not for you? Can you learn anything from the way this other person organizes?

7. **One system you wouldn't change at all.** Whether it's the way pots and pans are organized in the kitchen cupboards or the way files are arranged in an office file drawer, this is a system you've adapted to your styles. What do you like about it? Where/how else might you be able to use it, or something like it?

CHAPTER 5

T: Take Small Steps

For I, the Lord your God, hold
your right hand; it is I who say to you,
"Fear not, I will help you."
ISAIAH 41:13

Remember Gemma, the mom in chapter 1 who decided that the kids' rooms weren't the best place to start her organizational endeavors? As it turns out, she had the right idea. So often, when we want to get organized, we start with the most gargantuan project there is. Clean out the garage. Organize the attic. Go through every box in the basement.

No wonder we get frustrated.

You may remember that Gemma ended up back in the home office, the upstairs living space that was least in need of an intervention. She made a little progress, but she also fell prey to the downside of one of her styles, stashing the folder "somewhere" when it didn't fit where it belonged.

Sound familiar? If you had to estimate how many things are out of place in your home right this minute, would it be less than ten? Somewhere in the double digits? Over 100?

Don't do the math. But do consider this: Every item you pick up and put where it belongs (or get rid of altogether) is a step in the right direction. Taking small steps to getting organized has two parts: prevention and intervention.

How many times have you (like Gemma) just put something down on a flat surface (the desk, the kitchen counter, the dining room table) instead of putting it where it belongs? Don't beat yourself up — we've all done it! Unfortunately, the time we save in the moment isn't really saved time, it's just borrowed. We spend that banked time every time we need to put away the things we set down in a convenient spot. And when those single items accumulate to form a hot spot, we have clutter.

Fortunately, we can take small steps in lots of ways. We can take a single, simple step such as finally getting that bag of donations out of the trunk of the car and to its destination. We can tackle one spot, one drawer, or one shelf at a time until the whole area looks just the way we want it to. We can focus on finding a unique container and pressing it into service so it does double duty: creating a home for wayward items and looking pretty in the process. Or we can pick up as we go, concentrating on making things just a little bit better a little at a time. No matter the task, we can build on the foundation created by our strengths, continuing to do what works and using that information to troubleshoot what doesn't.

As mentioned earlier, there are two basic concepts at work when it comes to keeping things organized: prevention and intervention. Prevention is proactive; intervention is interactive. When we use prevention, we work to improve our habits so that, moving forward, our approach to organization will go more smoothly. We do this by replacing old patterns that led to piles and confusion with new habits that put our styles to work. This allows us to be proactive, keeping clutter and hot spots from forming in the first place.

What's a "hot spot"? Fly Lady (who also introduced me to organizing in short spurts) describes it as a spot that has the potential to grow from a small spark to a big mess, but I look at hot spots a little differently.[1] I see them as our drop zones – the places that are a little too convenient when it comes time to drop whatever it is we're holding: the kitchen counter, the dining room table, the top of the dresser in the bedroom.

When we tackle a hot spot, get rid of a tool or container that's not a match for our styles, or replace a dysfunctional system with one that's functional, we're using intervention, interacting directly with the organizational challenge in an effort to resolve a problem. Prevention keeps hot spots from forming in the first place. Intervention deals with the hot spots once they appear.

Most often, we need a combined approach. But no matter which steps we take, it's important to pay attention to the improvements we make. If that sounds suspiciously like what you read in chapter 4, you're right. Taking small steps can get us to our destination, but only if we start with the successes that allow us to recognize that we're on the right path. Every small step we

---

1. The Fly Lady, "What is a Hot Spot?," FlyLady.Net, accessed April 5, 2019, http://www.flylady.net/d/getting-started/fly-faq/#hotspot.

take is worth acknowledging — or even celebrating! — since small steps, especially those that put our styles to work, create big successes.

Let's take a look at two small steps we can take — one in the realm of prevention, the other an intervention.

DON'T PUT IT DOWN, PUT IT AWAY!

How many times have you caught yourself just putting something in the easiest, most available spot only to have to circle back later, pick it up, and put it away? Many of the styles, both personal and organizational, fall prey to this habit. If you have an *I need to see it* personal style, you're probably nodding knowingly — your entire system revolves around putting things down where you can see them! — whereas those with an *I love to be busy* organizational style might defensively (and accurately) claim that this happens only when they have too much to do. If your organizational style is *drop and run*, you might be like Isabelle in chapter 1, creating a path you can retrace to the exact spot where you dropped the item you're looking for. Those with an *I love stuff* personal style might set down new finds in any old spot until they find the "just right" home for them, while those with the *cram and jam* or *I know I put it somewhere* organizational styles might put things down/away temporarily in a convenient spot only, later on, to have trouble retrieving them in the same condition, or remembering where that "convenient spot" was.

See how easy it is for this habit to take hold? While changing this instinctive reaction won't instantly restore order, it will prevent piles from forming in the first place.

Owning up to this habit is the first step, but this comes with a caveat: Owning up and beating oneself up are *not* the same thing. As a *drop and run* organizer with an *I need to see it* personal style, I frequently have difficulty with this habit. Since I acknowledge that it creates clutter (which works at cross purposes to getting organized), I want to change.

That's it. Admission. No recrimination or self-flagellation. Yes, I do this. No, I don't want to keep doing it because it makes getting and staying organized unnecessarily difficult.

Next, determine a way to remind yourself *not* to do this. Make a sign or several signs and put them up in the places where you're most likely to fall prey to this habit. Or practice self-talk. Whenever you set something down, gently remind yourself that there's a better way. Say it aloud and say it matter-of-factly: **"Don't put it down, put it away!"** Or if you prefer, "Is this where this belongs?" That simple. Really.

Oh, you won't break the habit after making your signs or reminding yourself out loud once or twice, but, eventually, with time and desire to change, the new habit will replace the old one. After a while you won't even need to say it out loud anymore. I used to fall prey to this *drop and run* habit at least twice a week, dropping my bathrobe on the bed instead of hanging it in the closet (two steps away) when I was rushing to get ready for work. A soft reminder (**"Don't put it down, put it away!"**) to myself has made an impact. These days, when I'm tempted to drop my bathrobe on the bed or my mail onto the counter, a little voice inside my head says, **"Don't put it down, put it away!"** Gently and matter-of-factly, because if the voice gets too pushy, I tend to dig in my heels and drop it just because I can. But that's another story.

You don't have to be perfect (ever!) and you won't listen to that voice every time, especially at first. Remember, we're taking small steps here. But every single time you put something where it belongs instead of someplace else, you're improving your organizational skills, preventing clutter, and improving the overall look of the space, one item at a time. This one small change can help keep clear spaces clear, keep piles from forming, and cement a new habit — putting things away — that's at the center of a working organizational system.

Pretty powerful payoff for a simple change of habit. Take small steps indeed.

GIVE IT FIVE!

Where **Don't put it down, put it away!** is proactive and preventative, **Give it five!** is reactive and prescriptive — an intervention for a problem that already exists. For many of us, getting started on a project is the hardest part. When even the idea of starting feels overwhelming, we become experts at finding a multitude of other things to do instead. Then, not only does the project remain on our to-do list, but the longer we go without tackling it, the larger it looms. Sometimes it even gets bigger.

Give it five! is a strategy designed for just this situation. As self-explanatory as **Don't put it down, put it away!**, this tactic can, with the promise of a commitment of just five minutes, help us overcome that getting-started barrier. **Give it five!** is just as simple as it sounds. Choose a hot spot to work on. Set a timer for five minutes. Dig in. When the timer goes off, you have permission to stop.

Typically, one of two things happens at the end of five minutes. In some cases, joy, glee, and celebratory measures ensue because we've *finally* made some progress. We revel in the clear space we've created, marvel at the efficiency that enabled us to accomplish something (and have something to show for it) in just five minutes, and walk away satisfied.

Or perhaps we take a moment to do all those things, but then we *don't* walk away. Having successfully cleared the getting-started hurdle, we ride the momentum we've created and devote more time to the task at hand and, time permitting, we finish it. And then the celebration really kicks in because there's nothing like clear space where clutter once prevailed to jumpstart a celebration.

Some days, we'll have time and energy for only the first five minutes — or maybe we'll nudge five minutes to fifteen. Other days, we'll turn the timer off after five minutes, turn on some music, and show that hot spot who's boss. Either way, our goal is progress. Not only is progress a beautiful thing, but it's the philosophy that underlies the T in STYLE: Take small steps. Whether we're battling ubiquitous clutter or a succession of hot spots that seem to pop up over and over again, making progress is more important than achieving perfection. Life is busy, and just as our organizational challenges didn't arise overnight, they won't be easily (or permanently) swept away by one well-planned attack, no matter how long or enthusiastic it is. Each small step we take brings us closer to our destination: an organized, peaceful space that we can maintain with relative ease because it makes sense to us and is built on what we do naturally.

Simple as they are, **Don't put it down, put it away!** and **Give it five!** are powerful strategies. Not only are they easy and within reach for every style, they build habits and self-confidence. Many of us who've struggled to organize in traditional ways have had our confidence eroded by what feels like our failure to do something "everyone else" can manage so easily. But as I hope you've come to realize, organizing is a very personal act. Organizational success has everything to do with finding the right match between tools and styles, and nothing to do with our value as human beings. Some people find that match right away, embracing three-ring binders, pocket folders, and file cabinets and all they have to offer; others take more time and need to get creative in their approach. Either way, it's important to accept that any problems have more to do with the tools than the person using them. It's only when we find the right approach that organization actually comes close to being as easy as others make it look. And make no mistake: Some folks who make it look easy actually work very hard at making that happen.

Don't put it down, put it away! and **Give it five!** aren't the only small steps we can take. We can pick up as we go. We can choose one area and tackle it in several short (or not-so-short) sessions, especially for big areas like basements, attics, and garages. We can even play little games with ourselves, like setting a goal of picking up and putting away a certain number of items by the end of the day, or ridding ourselves of a certain number of items by a certain date. We can get creative, perhaps by using an old tool in a new way, customizing our approach, or re-creating our plan entirely.

And when we are finished, we can celebrate our success, congratulating ourselves on a job well done.

I'm sure many of you are wondering how this is enough. Maybe you're even certain I'm condoning laziness and sloth. *Five* minutes? *One* drawer? How will that make a dent in everything I need to do?

It will. But you're right, it's just a dent. I'm not suggesting that we attack one spot and then declare ourselves finished forever; but I am suggesting — no, endorsing — setting a succession of small goals. Success begets success. One small step after the other leads us to our destination. Every success we meet along the way increases our motivation, our confidence, and our *desire* to take that next step, so that eventually organizing isn't something we dread, just something we do. And when we press our styles into service, being organized becomes a part of who we are, and we feel good about the way we keep track of our things and our lives, maybe for the first time in a very long time.

As we move through the STYLE process, notice how each of these concepts builds on the others; none is sufficient in and of itself. Starting with successes is wonderful, but just that: a start. Focusing solely on successes keeps us from doing the trouble-shooting we need to do to take our organization to the next level. Taking small steps is great, but also plural; taking one small step isn't enough, but taking a bunch of them, armed with our styles and the ideas that arise when we stop feeling defeated and start following our styles, can lead us confidently in the direction of a system that works for us.

Because confidence is such an important ingredient in the organization process, these first two steps are confidence-builders as much as organization-builders. When we feel confident about our styles instead of embarrassed by them, we free ourselves to think creatively. This gives us the courage to abandon traditional tools and their uses and explore new ways of using what we have on hand, or daring to use something in a new way without caring about what anyone else thinks.

So, armed with your Style Sheet, choose a destination. What small step can you take to move forward on your organization journey?

KNOW THYSELF

My husband hates being stuck in traffic. I'm not a fan of this particular predicament either but, with age, I've learned to take a more philosophical approach, to believe I am where I'm meant to be.

Unless I'm in a hurry. Then all bets are off. And, as someone who struggles with one-more-thing-itis (I can do one more thing before I leave/run out of time!), I am often in a hurry.

Clearly, patience is not a gift with which I have been endowed. As a result, when I find myself growing irritated at red lights and chatty clerks and students who walk at a snail's pace because their faces are in their phones, I need to consciously pause and remind myself that I am where I am meant to be. I am where God has chosen to place me at this very moment, whether or not it makes sense to me. Accepting that I am where I am for a reason keeps me from wasting energy fighting a battle I can't win — one that makes me and everyone around me cranky and unpleasant in the process.

While it can be difficult to come to terms with progress that is slow, every small step takes us in the direction of something bigger. If we keep our goals in mind and set our sights on what matters, it's easy to keep moving in the right direction, even if it doesn't happen quickly. If we just keep moving forward, no matter the detours and construction delays, we'll arrive.

The combination of faith and consistent, small steps is a powerful one — and all the fuel we need to reach our most important destinations.

Smart organizers know when to ask for help.
Dear Lord, thank you for bringing me to an awareness of the small steps I take every day. As I approach this new organizing adventure, help me to focus more on what I do and less on what I leave undone. Help me to find the value in small steps and trust that those steps will, slowly and consistently, lead me on the path I desire while enabling me to enjoy more of this life you have given me. And, amid the small and large tasks in my day, help me to find joy in the people and gifts you have given me, no matter how imperfect. Amen.

LISA'S LISTS

Ten Small Steps to Get You Started

Organizing by STYLE is all about progress, and small steps are at the heart of progress.

Which of these might you start with, and what payoff can you enjoy as a result?

1. Put away one load of laundry.

2. Gather wayward items from one room and put them where they belong.

3. Clean out one drawer (*not* the junk drawer ... unless you must).

4. Sort through one pile of papers.

5. Clear off one flat surface.

6. Spend five minutes tackling a hot spot.

7. Turn one pile into a list and then put the pile away.

8. Make your bed.

9. Fold and put away and/or hang up clothing that isn't where it's supposed to be.

10. Complete one task you've been putting off.

CHAPTER 6

Y: Yes, It Has a Home

But you, take courage! Do not let your hands be weak, for your work shall be rewarded.
2 CHRONICLES 15:7

Piles. The one thing that stands (sometimes literally) between us and organization. Piles of papers, of toys, of clothing — you name it. Sometimes, these piles form because of habits like those we discussed in chapter 5. Or a shortage of time keeps us from getting things from where they are to where they belong. But for piles that persist, there is often a common denominator.

They consist of homeless items.

Okay, clearly they're not entirely homeless — they're in your home. But do they belong there? And if so, *where* in your home do they belong?

In organization, as in real estate, location is key. Where real-estate agents profess, "location, location, location," professional organizers remind us there's "a place for everything and everything in its place." As you can probably guess by this point in the book, I'm not here to crack the whip and make sure you put every last object in its place. I would be remiss, however, if I didn't give you some ideas on how to make this happen.

If you look back at the Putting Your Organizational Styles to Work planning pages in chapter 4, you might notice that the first line on every one of them begins with the same phrase: "Focus on establishing consistent homes for everything ... "

This is neither a typo nor the lazy way out. Every successful organizational system revolves around the concept of *logical* and *consistent* homes.

A logical home is one that

- is close to where the item is most often used;
- is the right size for the item; and
- takes into account how often the item needs to be accessed.

These guidelines lead us to store food in the pantry, toys in the playroom, and holiday decorations in the attic. They're also the reason we don't dedicate an entire kitchen drawer to a single pair of socks. One pair of socks doesn't need a drawer all to itself, and since we don't usually get dressed in the kitchen, it makes no sense to store socks there.

No matter how logical the home, however, all our planning does us no good if we don't put all this logic into practice. Good, style-based planning constitutes the logic in *logical* and *consistent*. If we don't regularly use the homes we've selected, or if we change our minds and put our things in different homes every time, we lack *consistency*. While putting something in a convenient place temporarily might make decluttering easy, it sets us up to struggle when we need to find that item again. Assigning logical homes helps us to put things away easily; consistent use of those logical homes helps us to retrieve items quickly. When we fail to do one or both of these things, it makes it hard to put things away, meaning our stuff is more likely to get left out and become — you guessed it:

Part of a pile.

When we talk about homes, we talk about two aspects: the larger place where we store something (the kitchen, the bedroom closet, the top shelf of the hall closet) and any subdivisions of these places, such as bins, boxes, baskets, and other containers. As always, your personal and organizational styles should set the parameters. A home isn't logical if it doesn't work for your styles, and your logical homes might not be logical to someone else, including others who share your living space. While we want to move away from literally cramming and jamming and dropping and running, we need to honor those tendencies as we select permanent homes for our things — especially those we use daily. We can do this by choosing homes that make it as easy to put things away as it is to put them down.

Let's take a look at some guidelines for selecting logical homes.

STORE THINGS WHERE YOU USE THEM ... OR DROP THEM ... OR NATURALLY PUT THEM

When you get the mail each day, where do you set it down? Your mail storage should be located as close as possible to that spot.

And it's not just mail. If we habitually put the same thing in the same place every time, that's consistency — one of the two ingredients we need to make organization work. Using the default drop spot as a designated home isn't laziness. It's style smarts in action. The easier we make it to put our things away, the more likely it is that we'll do just that, and our stuff will actually end up where it belongs.

So, take a quick look around your house. Which piles are exactly where they belong?

Are you shaking your head? Thinking I've lost mine? Certain it can't be this simple?

Okay, it's not always that simple. But the basic concept is.

When we store things where we normally drop them, we shorten the distance between putting something down and putting it away, which is key to creating an organizational system. If, however, the place you (or other family members) drop things is a flat surface used for other purposes (kitchen counter, dining room table, family-room floor), it might not be the ideal home.

But it's a start. Remember that the goal is to establish a system that's easy to use and easy to maintain because it's true to your styles. Creating new habits is much harder than tweaking the ones we already have; making small adjustments in what we naturally do is much easier than starting from scratch.

I fought the mail battle for a long time and, the truth was, I was the culprit. I'd come into the house with my hands full and I'd dump the mail. And then I'd get busy, and the mail would stay exactly where I left it, accumulating over time. I tried baskets, bins, and a variety of pretty containers, but I was never satisfied because, in the end, the mail was still there, taking up space on an otherwise clear counter.

But since I really didn't have another place to put the mail, I needed to find containers and a system that suited my styles *and* that had a small enough footprint not to interfere with my (mostly) clear counter. Once I found the right fit (after much trial and error, I must admit), I was motivated to make sure the mail went where it belonged, as opposed to being strewn across the counter, on a daily basis. Now, most days, I sort the mail as I come in, put the things to be filed into an open file bin on the counter (my final solution), and divvy the rest up by recipient. You might say the mail, my styles, and I achieved a compromise that worked for all of us.

Another important consideration here is who is using the system. Once upon a time, I set up the bins in my bathroom cabinets in a way that worked for me. The system was logical and, as a bonus, the bins all matched and looked pretty.

The problem? I wasn't the one using the bins. My daughter was. Or wasn't, most of the time, as her stuff ended up on the bathroom counter instead of in the cabinet.

Initially, I was annoyed by the clutter. Then I realized that the clutter was a clue. If I adjusted the system, placing the bins where she usually stashed her stuff, we might both live happily ever after, at least as far as bathroom storage was concerned.

Where do you (or other people living in your house) drop stuff? Can you put a bin or a hook or some other organizer there (or nearby) to collect the clutter? This may or may not be a long-term solution, but containment is a great place to start, and something we'll talk about in a little more detail later in this chapter.

STORE THINGS THAT ARE USED EVERY DAY IN PLACES THAT ARE EASY TO ACCESS

"Easy" should be defined by the styles and attributes of the person who most often uses the item. I'm five feet tall, my daughter is five-eight and my husband is six feet tall. Easy access will clearly be defined differently for each of us. I can use top shelves and out-of-the-way cabinets to store things I need only once in a while, but if I store things I use every day in those out-of-reach locations, I'll never put anything away. The inaccessibility of the shelves combined with my *I need to see it* personal style will override any desire to put things away (and out of sight).

When we remodeled our kitchen, we splurged on two things I love to this day. The first is a Lazy Susan cupboard that uses the dead space in the corner between the dishwasher and the stove; the second is a set of slide-out shelves inside the lower cabinets. Much of what I use regularly goes in those two spots — and gets put away when I'm finished because it's easy to access the spot. And because spinning the Lazy Susan or pulling open the drawer makes everything visible, I don't feel the need to keep things out where I can see them. Once things are away, finding and accessing them again is as easy as opening a cabinet door.

But just because it's accessible doesn't mean it's logical. When I taught the concept of logical homes to my elementary-school students, I asked them to imagine they'd just returned from a trip to a warehouse store like Costco, BJ's, or Sam's Club. As they unloaded everything they (or their parents) had purchased, they managed to find homes for everything except a large multi-pack of toilet paper. Since it was too big to stash anywhere in its wrapped state, they'd need to open it up and put away individual rolls. After storing some of the rolls in the bathroom and putting most of the rest in a nearby closet, they still had several rolls that needed to be put somewhere. Desperate, they returned to the kitchen, opened the oven door, and, finding the oven empty, decided to stash the remaining rolls of toilet paper in the oven.

Needless to say, even ten-year-olds recognized the foolishness of this decision.

While I doubt that any of you routinely use your oven as storage for toilet paper, I suspect that there's at least one item in your house that's stored in an out-of-the-way or illogical place simply because that's where there was room. And if you have an *I know I put it somewhere* organizational style, chances are that's the rule rather than the exception. Understanding that something doesn't belong where it is the first step. Finding a more accessible location is a tad more complicated but, in the long run, worth the effort. When the locations we choose are accessible, putting things away isn't so hard.

But just because something is easy to put away doesn't make it easy to retrieve. Even the most easily accessible locations don't guarantee easy retrieval for every style. My husband, who has an *I know I put it somewhere* organizational style, loves filing cabinets, so all his papers go into one of his filing cabinets (yes, he has more than one). This makes both access and retrieval easy for him; since nearly all his papers end up in one of the filing cabinets (somewhere), he needs to look in only one place to find the paper he's looking for.

Although, as someone with an *I need to see it* personal style, I agree that file cabinets are accessible, but I gave up on them long ago — at least when it comes to using them to store things I need to use on a regular basis. For me, there's little functional difference between a file cabinet and a trash can. Yes, the file cabinet is better organized, and I can color-code my files by general topic, but unless I create a more visual filing system (one that's out in the open, not inside a closed drawer), my papers end up in piles where I can see them — on my desk or on the dining-room table. A file cabinet just can't compete with that kind of access, so it's important to ...

CHOOSE A STORAGE SOLUTION (CONTAINER AND LOCATION) THAT MAKES PUTTING THINGS AWAY AS EASY AS PUTTING THEM DOWN

How often have you set something aside to put away later because putting it where it belongs is too complicated or time-consuming? That's a sure sign that the place where it's currently stored might not be the right home for it. Making putting something away as easy as simply putting it down is a key step in the organization process.

Frequently used items should get prime real estate — that's why the clean sheets we need weekly go on the most accessible shelves of the linen closet, but the thick, woolen blankets go on the top shelf. The less often you use something, the more out-of-the-way it can be stored. (There's a reason we store seasonal items in the attic and the garage, often on high shelves.) And as we discussed earlier, if we can choose a location that's close to where we naturally put (or drop) things, we're less likely to put things down and more likely to put them away.

With three of our concepts down, let's bring them into our living space. Look around and find an item — or maybe even a pile of items — that's out of place. Turn off any blame (including self-blame) and look at the item(s) analytically.

- Do these items have a home, or are they homeless?
- If they have a home, is it logical and accessible?
- How did they land where they are right now? Can they stay there?
- Is the problem where their home is located, or what they're stored in?

The questions above crystallize the three concepts we've just discussed when it comes to settling on homes for our things: the location itself, its accessibility, and how easy or complicated it is to get things to the places we've assigned. All these are questions of logistics.

As we move from larger spaces to their smaller subdivisions, we begin to mingle logistics and aesthetics. When we talk about homes that are logical, consistent, and accessible, we're talking about logistics. When we talk about choosing the right container to house or subdivide our belongings, we're bringing aesthetics into the picture.

A stack of mail on the counter may be logistically acceptable as long as we can still access the counter, but is it aesthetically pleasing? That's another story.

As we discuss our last two location concepts, we'll consider both logistics and aesthetics.

STORE SIMILAR ITEMS TOGETHER

Logistically, this is easy enough, but let's begin with an example that utilizes large, rectangular spaces we have throughout our homes: closets and drawers. Fill in the blank: All coats and outerwear belong in _____.

Easy enough? Okay. Let's define "outerwear." Coats and jackets, certainly. Hats, gloves, scarves, mittens? Sure. Boots? Okay. That big, heavy blanket you use outside at the fire pit or when you go tailgating? For the sake of argument, let's include that, too.

Now imagine all these things tossed haphazardly into the space you've specified — which, if it's anything like mine, houses other items too. The logistics make sense. All outwear belongs together.

But how much togetherness is too much? At what point does all that togetherness become an amorphous blob that gets knotted together by mitten strings and shoelaces? Not a pretty picture.

You're probably one step ahead of me here, having already subdivided the large, rectangular space that's housing all this outerwear and having separated the mittens from the boots.

And that, my friends, is the sweet spot where logistics meet aesthetics.

Now let's put the logic in logistics. If you've accessed the space that houses all the outerwear, and everyone can find, reach, and easily grab everything they need, go pour yourself a beverage and finish reading this chapter from the comfort of your couch.

If one or more of those pieces is missing, you, like me, will most likely be standing in front of this space wondering how to improve it. You can do that if you wish, or you can take a mental (or actual) picture, grab a beverage, and finish this chapter from the comfort of your couch.

But before we forge ahead, let's flip back. Take a look at your Style Sheets and the Containers Chart at the end of part I. When it comes to choosing the right container, what do your styles tell you? Keep some of the overall concepts in mind as you approach the remainder of this chapter.

One of the strategies that can increase the accessibility of a space is subdividing, and containers can help us accomplish that. They can be purely practical (repurposed boxes, clear plastic drawers, shelf dividers, for example) or they can be pretty and practical (matching storage boxes, unique containers, bins with family members' names embroidered on them, to name a few), but they still need to be logical, accessible, and a fit for the styles of everyone who will use them. Let's consider this together with the final location concept.

CHOOSE A SPACE THAT'S THE RIGHT SIZE

This is the Goldilocks rule. The homes we choose should have enough room for the item to fit without getting crumpled, broken, or torn, but not so much room that things get lost in them and/or space is wasted by the footprint of the container. Think of it as you'd think of buying clothes for a young child: The clothes should fit, but not so tightly that there's no room to grow. Choose containers that are the right size for what you currently own, with a little space for future acquisitions.

Let's go back (mentally) to the closet housing our outerwear. Because this is at its heart a big, rectangular space, storage is maximized when we section it off. Imagine, for a moment, an empty closet. What do you see?

Nearly every closet comes equipped with at least one shelf and at least one rod or closet system that creates hanging space. This not only subdivides the closet but suggests functions for each area of the closet.

Take a moment and consider your styles and the size of the place where you are storing outerwear (or, if that's in good shape, think about your bedroom closet or any other large, rectangular space). How is it already subdivided? Are those subdivisions working? What would you add or subtract?

The answer to the last two questions depends on your styles, as well as the function you want that space to serve. In other words, what are you storing there, and what's the best way to do that, based on your styles and the location concepts we've discussed in this chapter?

To answer these questions, we need to consider form, function, and style. Despite their variation in appearance, all containers, whether large and rectangular or small and cute, have just three components: form, function and style. *Form* refers to the size, shape, and physical attributes of a container, including features such as lids and sections (and doors). *Function* is exactly what it sounds like — the purpose the container serves. A container's *style* comes from its aesthetics — color, texture, pattern, and attractiveness.

All these attributes matter. How *much* each one matters depends on what needs to go into the container and — you guessed it — the personal and organizational styles of the person (or people) using it. Aesthetics may seem superficial, but often, choosing a container we truly like for reasons of both decorative style and personal/organizational style makes the difference between using it and not using it.

Your mission will be to try to find containers that will help you to create systems that are both appealing and functional. This is where your Style Sheets and Container Charts can help. The containers you choose may be the storage solution themselves, or they may be tools to subdivide a larger space to make it easier to find small items in a big space.

You might have noticed that when I use the term "container," I use it broadly, referencing everything from closets, drawers, and file cabinets to bins, boxes, and binders. For some ideas about container attributes to consider, check out the Lisa's List at the end of this chapter.

Finally, let's go back to the large, rectangular space housing our outerwear one last time. Because this is a dynamic space, especially in cold weather, organizing this space and keeping it that way will be a process. Like my bathroom bin setup, this space has to suit everyone who uses it; otherwise, it will become littered with clutter-based clues. To save yourself from headaches later, set it up now with input from its users. Perhaps you'll come up with a plan and then run it by your family for feedback, or perhaps you'll choose to seek their feedback up front.

Wait a minute. If you're doing all the work, can't you just tell everyone where to put everything?

Sure. I mean, look how well that worked for me with my bathroom bins.

While it's certainly your prerogative to lay down the law about shared spaces, if you're truly Organizing by STYLE, that means understanding that your styles may differ from other people's. My daughter and I both have *drop and run* organizational styles, but my husband is an *I know I put it somewhere* organizer through and through. His need to put things away is at odds with my *I need to see it* personal style (which feeds my *drop and run* organizational style), so if one of us sets up a system based on our preferred styles and expects the other to use it, we're likely to be very disappointed, to say the least.

Accommodating another person's style doesn't mean you

have to give up your own. The bathroom bins my daughter bypassed (until I moved them) worked for my husband because there was plenty of space for him to store his stuff and the precise location was up to him. People with an *I know I put it somewhere* organizational style can use logical homes — in fact, they often crave them — so their systems can coexist with systems that work for *drop and run* or *cram and jam* organizers. The trick is to find commonalities among the preferences embodied by each style so that we can create systems that enable everyone to put their things not down, but away.

Overwhelmed? That's understandable. Once you've identified your styles, a lot of this is trial and error — and that's for just *one* person. Mixing and matching the styles of everyone in a family takes time and patience. As we press forward, keep in mind that this is a process and not something you will accomplish in an afternoon, or even a weekend. You're likely to make mistakes and misjudgments along the way, and it may take more than one try to get a particular hot spot whipped into shape (Exhibit A: my mail counter). Be patient with yourself and with those around you. And when you find something that works, stick to your guns and, perhaps more important, try to replicate it in other spaces.

Over time, I've found a small arsenal of tools that work for me and my *I need to see it/drop and run* styles. Few of my containers have lids. Most are colorful, brightly colored, unique, or labeled. Each of the containers that works for me works because it makes it as easy for me to put something away as to put it down. If you share my styles, you might like these tools as well, or you may have a completely different set of preferences. The styles are merely a starting point for creating individualized systems that work for the people who need to use them.

Ready to put some of this knowledge to work? Let's start with a container you already have. Choose one you love or, alternatively, one you'd like to replace. Or, if you wish, you can go back to the outerwear storage space we've been analyzing so far. Then, using the chart on the next page, assess the container you've chosen. I've done a sample to get you started. As you can see, there may be some overlap between what you like/dislike and what works/doesn't, but there might also be some attributes that you simply like, even if they play no role in the function of the container.

All this information is important. There are several objectives at work here: determining what you like/dislike from an aesthetic perspective, determining what you like/dislike based on your styles, examining the attributes of a container, analyzing how these attributes work (or don't), and determining whether or not a container is earning its keep.

	Container	Mail file
How valuable is it?	What I like/ dislike about it	Attractive, open on top so I can see what's inside & access the contents easily.
	Why it works/Why it doesn't	Contents are visible & easily accessible; container has a small footprint, so I can keep most of the counter clear.
Keep or replace?	Keep?	Yes!
	Replace it with a container that ...	Not replacing! Finally found a keeper for this spot/task.

	Container		
How valuable is it?	What I like/dislike about it		
	Why it works/ Why it doesn't		
Keep or replace?	Keep?		
	Replace it with a container that ...		

Seems like a tall order for a little chart, doesn't it? Since this part of the process, more than any other, is very much trial and error, looking at containers from multiple angles can help us to quickly make decisions about what's worth trying in the first place. Sometimes we don't know what we want, and this chart can help narrow that down. Other times we know exactly what we want but can't find it anywhere. We know what the standard tools look like and how they function; if we can analyze what we want that those tools don't have, we're on the way to creating individualized systems that have a style (in the traditional sense) all their own. Combining the chart above and Lisa's List at the end of this chapter with the Container Chart, your Style Sheets, and your own personal taste, you can begin to get a sense of what will work for you consistently.

Now let's play. I can't stress enough that there's no one right answer here, and that you don't always have to use a container for its intended purpose. This is the part where creativity and ingenuity come into play — the part where it gets fun. Since both creativity and ingenuity emerge much more easily when we're patient with ourselves, approaching container selection playfully helps us to tap into those talents. Armed with the conclusions from your charts and Style Sheets, go window shopping to see what's out there that might solve a storage dilemma or cool off a hot spot where clutter collects.

Keep in mind that *this is a process*, and processes take time. The goal here is to start with successes so that you can keep — and replicate — the things you're doing well, while also looking for new ideas that fit your styles and take things to the next level. Brainstorm. Try something new. Assess its value and keep it, replace it and/or replicate it. You're the boss.

Slowly, one success, one home, and one container at a time, you'll build a system designed just for you.

But first, let's make sure all that stuff you have is worth storing in the first place.

KNOW THYSELF

I've spent nearly all my adult life as a Pennsylvanian, but I will forever identify as a Jersey girl. I attribute this to several things, with the bad rap New Jersey gets from hordes of people who've never even been there and my own stubbornness topping the list. After my mom passed away, my dad moved to Pennsylvania to be closer to my sister and me, leaving me no real reason to "go home." I have to admit, that makes me a little sad.

Homes are important. They provide warmth, comfort, and stability, and shape who we become. While the homes we se-lect for our belongings have simpler requirements and can be changed more easily, they serve to protect the things that matter to us. If it's worth keeping, it's worth taking care of. God calls us to be faithful and prudent stewards of all that he has given us, after all, to tend to our belongings, our homes, and our relation-ships.

Within the home that you have built, how will you be a good steward? How will you protect and respect all that God has provided?

Smart organizers know when to ask for help.
Dear Lord, thank you for a home filled with beautiful things and places to put them. The process of finding logical, consistent homes for everything I own feels daunting. Walk with me as I take things one step at a time, and endow me with the patience necessary to understand and cherish the styles of those around me. Amen.

LISA'S LISTS

Eight Container Attributes
to Mix and Match

What do you do when your styles call for different container types? Mix and match, of course!

1. Clear

2. Colored — tinted or opaque

3. Lidded

4. Unlidded (a.k.a. topless)

5. Solid (wood, brass, plastic, and other unyielding materials)

6. Flexible (fabric, woven, bendable, or stretchy)

7. Unique (one-of-a-kind, handcrafted, of an interesting shape or design)

8. Handled/portable (totes)

CHAPTER 7

L: Let It Go!

God loves a cheerful giver.
2 Corinthians 9:7

Depending upon your styles, you're either zooming in on this chapter with enthusiasm or considering skipping it altogether. For some of us, even the thought of getting rid of our belongings is emotionally daunting (yes, my *I love stuff* friends, this means you). We can become a little defensive — maybe even a little annoyed — at the mere prospect of someone else telling us how easy it is to simply ditch everything we love in the name of tidiness.

C'mon. Don't you know me better than that by now? This book isn't about mere tidiness or ditching everything we love. It's about organizing in a way that works for you, and that means finding homes for the things you love, not tossing them out just to make the job simpler.

But, if we're being honest here, we need to acknowledge that the less stuff we have, the easier it is to keep everything organized. I'm reminded of our beach vacations where suddenly life clicks into place and things look tidy (okay, my little corner of things does anyway). Of course it does! Ninety percent of my stuff is still at home! It's not hard at all to take control of 10 percent of my stuff.

Ah, but the other 90 percent. There's the sticking point.

Making sure that everything we have is worth keeping is an important part of getting organized. By extension, that means letting go of the things we no longer need, use, or have room for. Type A organizers are particularly good at this; however, if you're reading this book, I suspect you, like me, find this process challenging at least some of the time. Keeping that in mind, I'll attempt to move forward as painlessly as possible, with a sense of love and respect for all my friends who are cringing at the mere mention of downsizing. But move forward I must, since the best (and easiest) way to reduce clutter is to eliminate what's unnecessary.

Let's start by listing some things pretty much everyone would agree fit the definition of unnecessary:

- Things that are broken, torn, shredded and/or

beyond repair
- Things that are missing pieces
- Half of a pair of anything
- Things that are time sensitive, but hopelessly out of date
- Things past their stated expiration date

Anything you'd add?

Now, let's dig a little deeper. Here are a few things that are a tad more controversial:

- Anything (besides a uniform or special occasion garment) that hasn't been worn in more than a year
- Out-of-style or uncomfortable clothing or shoes
- Anything that's been waiting to be repaired for more than six months or a season, whichever is more appropriate
- Outgrown clothing that can't be handed down to someone else within the next month (again, there are exceptions)
- Duplicates, triplicates, or quadruplicates (or more) of a nonconsumable item (how many potato peelers do we need?)
- Anything that's been replaced with a newer, better version, unless both are still being used (multiple crock pots, for example)
- Children's artwork that is more than ten years old (reduce collection by 90 percent)
- Duplicate photographs that cannot be shared with another person within the next month
- Any catalog that's available online

How are you doing? Anyone hyperventilating yet?

While I expect that a few of the items above will elicit a

"yes, but … " response, approaching your stuff with even half of these guidelines in mind can help even the most determined *I love stuff* person begin the downsizing process. And as we discussed in chapter 5, getting started is often the most difficult part. Guidelines (like **Give it five!** for example) can give us the framework that helps us to dig in.

If this list has motivated you to look scavenger-hunt style for items that fit the descriptions, scavenge away! The remainder of the chapter will be here waiting when you return.

More overwhelmed than motivated? Let's find a starting point for each style. The personal and organizational styles are listed in the next chart, along with a suggested starting point for each one. Find your styles and choose the one (personal or organizational) whose starting point feels more approachable to you.

Prefer the starting point for another style? Have at it! Anything that gets you started is fair game, especially if this is a tough task for you.

Style	Choose ...	Actions
I love to be busy	a container that houses the supplies for one of your activities	dump and sort
I love stuff	a container that houses a variety of "stuff"	dump and sort
I need to see it	a pile, any pile	turn it over and start sorting from the bottom
Cram & jam	any fully stuffed container	dump and sort
I know I put it somewhere	open a drawer or find a "safe" place	remove contents and sort from the bottom of the pile
Drop & run	a path or a pile	approach the path from either direction, sorting as you go or sort from the bottom of the pile

Why, you might ask, am I sorting from the bottom of the pile? Because the items on the bottoms of piles are usually older than those on top. Often, it's easier to make decisions about those items, especially if they're expired and/or you've forgotten all about them.

How, you might ask, am I supposed to sort? Begin by creating three piles: keep, don't keep, and I don't know. If you opt to keep something, you need to find it a home in the next twenty-four hours. Items in the "I don't know" pile can be set aside for now, but you need to set a deadline of one week or less for making a final decision and moving it into one of the other piles.

Things that go into a "don't keep" pile can be assigned a variety of destinations. The most obvious answer is to toss these items in the trash or recycling bin, but obvious isn't synonymous with easy. For lots of people, particularly those with an *I love stuff* personal style, getting rid of a beloved item can feel like letting go of a piece of oneself.

Fortunately, throwing things away isn't the only way to clear the clutter — unless you're talking about something that poses a health hazard, like, say, a week's worth of banana peels. Anything that invites unwelcome visitors of the insect or rodent variety should be disposed of. Quickly.

But not all "don't keep" decisions are that easy. When my daughter was small, she was firmly entrenched in the *I love stuff* personal style, and no logic or reason could get her to toss or recycle something before she was ready. But if we could pass the item in question along to someone else who'd enjoy it, she was much more willing to let it go. Over time, my daughter has become a lot more ruthless when it comes to decluttering, but this isn't true for everyone. Some folks have a strong, lifelong *I love stuff* personal style. For those who remain true-blue *I love stuff* thinkers, recycling, reselling, and repurposing can be valid alternatives to the trash can when it's time to **Let it go!**

Let's take these options one at a time. When it comes to recycling, we need to think outside the bin to the broadest possible definition of recycling: giving new life to old things. When we think of it in those terms, it's about more than just tossing a rinsed-out soda bottle into the recycling container. It can be about finding new homes for things we've loved but no longer need, like my daughter did. Donating, consigning, and even having yard sales fit into this expanded definition of recycling.

And donating goes far beyond church rummage sales and clothing collection boxes. Did you know you can recycle blue jeans? Mail that plastic hotel key you brought home by mistake to a place where it can be melted down and made into ... more plastic hotel keys? Donate the reusable grocery bags that seem to overrun your car when you don't need them but hide from you when you do? Type "donate wedding dress," "donate business clothes," or "donate prom dress" into a search engine and you'll find a page (or more) of local and national organizations that will put those items into the hands of people who need them. While I'm not ready to donate my wedding gown (unpreserved though it may be) any time soon, I'm more than happy to let go of that bridesmaid's dress I most definitely did not wear again.

Wondering what to do with other household items? Homeless shelters and animal shelters will often be happy to take old sheets and towels off your hands. The St. Vincent de Paul Society takes a wide variety of household items. I regularly take bags full of books to our local library (it's the only way I can make room for new ones!). Some they keep, others they sell to raise money to buy more books for their collection. Either way, I'm contributing to a collection that serves many people who can enjoy the books as much as or perhaps more than I did.

Do you have something you're ready to get rid of, but have no idea how to find it a new home? Look online for ideas.[2] I was amazed by the number of things that can be reused and repurposed.

Feeling gratified by the idea of finding new homes for your things but thinking all that stuff in your basement might earn enough for a weekend getaway? You're not alone. For some of us, nothing short of the lure of cold, hard cash can soothe the ache that accompanies getting rid of our "stuff." I have friends who consider yard sales a win/win: They free up space while simultaneously getting back some of the money they invested in their things as well.

I'm not really a yard sale girl, but I love consigning things, especially clothes. I pack up the things we've outgrown, grown tired of, or never should have bought in the first place, and take

2. Lori Brown, "Wow, You Can Recycle That?," Earth911, February 8, 2010, https://earth911.com/home/wow-you-can-recycle-that/.

them to a local shop that sells them and then cuts me a check. In the meantime, if I want to buy something there, I can spend the credit I've accumulated (between the time they sell my things and the time they cut the check) instead of spending cash, which makes me feel like I'm getting something for free. If I resist the urge to shop and stay out of the store between drop-offs (which I typically do twice a year), the credit keeps accumulating until the end of the consignment period when a check lands in my mailbox.

Most clothing consignment stores accept only a season or two at a time, so it's wise to call ahead and find out what guidelines, if any, they have. The consignment stores I use accept spring and summer clothes beginning in January and fall and winter clothes beginning in June. I keep two boxes in my laundry area so I can move things right from my dryer to either the spring/summer box or the fall/winter box. This plan keeps me from putting the clothes back in my closet where they might take up permanent residence.

Depending on where you live, it might be possible to consign more than just clothing. Some consignment stores in our area accept and sell furniture and household items, and one sells sporting goods. Again, it's wise to call ahead to find out what they accept and what their policy is. I want to know that once something is out of my house, it's out for good, so I look for stores that offer the option to donate unsold merchandise.

To me, consignment is the perfect combination of reselling and recycling. I drop everything off in one place. I earn some money, but I don't have to sit outside for hours on a hot, humid Pennsylvania day and bargain with strangers. And if the things don't sell, they're donated to someone who might be able to use them.

But as far as I'm concerned, the biggest benefit of consigning is that once I make the decision to let something go, I don't have to think about it again. I drop it off at the consignment shop, and they take it from there. This makes it much less likely that I'll change my mind because, in order to do that, I'd have to buy it back or hope it remains unsold so I can claim it again after the consignment period is up, both of which defeat the purpose.

If you'd like to make recycling or reselling a part of your routine, it's helpful to take your styles into consideration as you choose the containers you'll use as temporary holding zones for the items you want to consign. As someone with an *I need to see it* personal style, I need containers that are open on top and labeled, so I can see which season is in which box. This works for my *drop and run* organizational style too; unless I choose containers that are open and accessible, it's easier to put things back into the laundry basket than it is to put them into the consignment box. Still, there is something to be said for closing the lid on the box once you've made the decision to part with something.

*Cram and jam*mers need to have containers large enough to keep them from, well, cramming and jamming, as many consignment stores are particular about the condition of the clothing they accept. And *I know I put it somewhere* organizers will benefit from containers that are clear, labeled, or color-coded and have a specific home, so that when it's time to take things to the consignment store, they can remember (or see) where they put the things they wanted to take. Those with an *I love to be busy* personal style might want to put their containers into the trunk of the car as soon as they're full to fit a drop-off more easily into their busy schedules. This can be true for those with an *I love stuff* personal style as well, since the sooner the stuff is out of the house, the more likely the decision to part with it will stand.

And then there are those who, halfway to the consignment container, donation in hand, suddenly see a new way of using that tchotchke, basket, tablecloth, glass jar, or piece of clothing. These are the folks for whom repurposing can be a valid alternative to letting things go, provided that moderation prevails and their collection of things to repurpose doesn't take on a life of its own. Judicious use of three concepts we've already discussed can help to ensure that the "to be repurposed" pile is fun-sized. The things that are being rescued for repurposing need a location, a deadline, and a just-right container. (That's *one* container, not a pile of them.) Whatever you're saving to repurpose needs to find a home (at least a temporary one) within twenty-four hours. Here are a few questions to ask yourself as you consider deadlines and container size:

- **Is this item worth the space it takes up?** If not, the answer should be easy.

- **Do I already have a place to put this between now and when I plan to use it?** If so, save away. If not, take a look at the remaining questions before making a final decision. If the space you plan to use to store the item is full, get rid of something else before adding this new treasure to the collection.

- **How often do I engage in repurposing?** If you are someone who repurposes regularly (no less than once a month), it's not a problem if you save more stuff, especially if you already know where it's going to go until you get to it. If you have lots of great ideas for repurposing, but rarely get around to actually carrying them out, go back to question #1.

- **When do I think I will get to this?** If it will take you more than a month to actually get back to this item and your great idea for reusing it, rethink the decision to repurpose. Allowable exceptions exist for seasonal projects (if you find something in April you want to repurpose for Christmas, for example) and projects you anticipate getting to during a scheduled vacation or time off. Once you decide on this time frame, label the item(s) to be repurposed with a date. If you get to that date and haven't used the items, it's time to let them go.

For this task as for all the others, I stand by my (consistent) assertion that one approach does not fit all. Only you can decide what's trash and what's treasure, and you're bound to end up with some things you simply can't let go of — yet. The idea is to make sure that pile of keepers is as small and meaningful as possible. There's a certain ruthlessness to thinning the piles of stuff, and it can take multiple passes through the same pile before we fully engage, or even find, our ruthlessness.

What if you're not ruthless at all? If you struggle to get rid of anything, or to let others do so on your behalf, it's possible that you're dealing with something more challenging than trying to find the right approach to organization. I'm not a medical professional, and no book is a substitute for a clinical diagnosis, so it's impossible to determine just from reading these pages whether or not something deeper is at work. But, if you're worried about an inability to let things go, the section below might help you determine whether you should talk to a medical professional about your concerns.

HOARDING

Most of us struggle to get rid of some of our things some of the time. Usually, we have an emotional connection with the item, and keeping it is more about the memories and feelings evoked than the thing itself. These items tend to be the exception rather than the rule, and, in most situations, we can reliably distinguish trash from treasure. While most of us who love stuff are what our grandmothers referred to as "pack rats," for others the problem goes deeper.

Compulsive hoarding is defined by the International OCD Foundation as ALL THREE of the following:

1. A person collects and keeps a lot of items, even things that appear useless or of little value to

most people.

2. These items clutter the living spaces and keep the person from using their rooms as they were intended.

3. These items cause distress or problems in day-to-day activities.[3]

How do we know if we should be concerned? Let me begin with the emphasis placed on ALL THREE (capital letters theirs) and the word "*and*" (italics mine). I cannot stress enough that *all these* criteria must be met. If you are "simply" a collector or "simply" have a cluttered living space, that does not make you a hoarder.

Hoarding is distinguished by a pattern of symptoms that causes distress for the person experiencing them, but it's treatable. Tough love and forced removal of beloved objects can sometimes cause more harm than good, and appropriate treatment typically requires more than simply advice on how to get organized.

Why do people hoard? It could be personality or family history. Or it could be triggered by a stressful life event. Sometimes it's connected to anxiety, depression, or obsessive-compulsive disorder.

It's possible for any one of us to show symptoms of hoarding. But clinical hoarding, like any other clinical disorder, is typified by a *pattern of symptoms* — not just a few isolated symptoms that ebb and flow with stress and busyness.

If you've been successfully making progress with your organizational systems, even slowly, you're probably not a hoarder.

If you understand that other people don't see the same value

---

3. Christiana Bratiotis, PhD, et al., International OCD Foundation, https://iocdf.org /wp-content/uploads/2014/10/Hoarding-Fact-Sheet.pdf.

in certain objects that you do, and you can distinguish true trash from true treasure, you're probably not a hoarder.

If prior to purchasing the super-jumbo family pack at the warehouse club you ask yourself where you're going to put it when you get it home, you're probably not a hoarder.

If you have surfaces that collect clutter, but you can still move through your home and use the rooms and appliances for the purposes for which they're intended, you're probably not a hoarder.

If, however, anything here has you concerned, please visit the website for the International OCD Foundation. There, you'll find a clear document that distinguishes common, non-clinical behaviors from those that are more concerning.

At the end of the day (or week or month), will there still be things in your home that others (and maybe even you) deem frivolous, silly, or unnecessary? I certainly hope so. Our aim here is not an ascetic lifestyle but rather one where we can find what we need when we need it in a home that is warm and welcoming and that boasts a few treasures that make us smile. Judiciously letting go of the things you don't need creates space to let the things you love shine.

KNOW THYSELF

This morning, as I was getting dressed, I put on one of the long necklaces I bought to accessorize plain sweaters. I kept it on for a little while, but eventually took it off, exchanging it for something daintier so that I could wear the "statement" earrings I love.

I have at least four of those long necklaces, each a bit different from the other, and I have been through this put-on-take-off ritual more times than I can count. Only once did the necklace actually make it out of the house.

The necklaces, while lovely, weigh me down. They make me wish I were taller or slimmer or less well-endowed, rather than being content with who I am and how I actually look.

Those statement earrings? I'd wear them every day if I could. They're fun, lightweight, and a little jingly; and, when I wear them, I feel fun and breezy, too. They don't simply accessorize my outfit; they let the best of me shine through.

I know that no possession can define who I am — nor should it. We're not meant to store up earthly treasures, so we should be discerning about the things we keep, always making sure that our external treasures have at least as much substance as sparkle. Our task, then, is to truly appreciate the things we keep, aware that we have all of them through the goodness of a generous and loving God.

What do your treasures represent to you?

Smart organizers know when to ask for help.

Dear Lord, thank you for the many physical blessings you have brought into my life. Help me to discern those that might benefit others and to let go of things that are just taking up space. Help me to appreciate the things I keep and to acquire new belongings purposefully, with an eye for beauty and utility rather than mere acquisition. Amen.

LISA'S LISTS

Let It Go Habits to Develop, One at a Time

Do you find **Let It Go!** to be the hardest step in the STYLE process?

Here are a few tips for incorporating it into daily life.

1. **Let it go before you set it down.** Go through the mail, extraneous receipts (things you've paid cash for and won't be returning), and any other kind of easily disposable items before you give them even a temporary spot in your home. Make a list of items you can do this with, and post it where it will remind you.

2. **One in, one out.** When you bring something new home, get rid of something old. This works well with replacements for similar items (replace that old white blouse that's closer to gray with the new one you just bought), but can also be used with unrelated items of similar size.

3. **Set a limit on the number of items in a single category (e.g., tablecloths) that you'll allow yourself to accumulate.** This number should be based on how often the items get used. In other words, if you don't use a different tablecloth each week, fifty-two tablecloths is excessive.

4. **Keep no more than two spare packages of any one item.** We all have those items we don't want to run out of, so keeping a spare package

is good planning. Keeping more than two spare packages (spare being beyond what you're likely to use in a week, or between regular shopping trips) can set the stage for storage problems.

5. **Put things in order by expiration date.** Keeping the oldest items on the top of the pile or in the front of the cabinet helps to reduce waste as well as the disappointment that arises when you discover that you actually *don't* have that ingredient you thought you did. In addition, it's relatively easy to see what needs to be thrown away.

6. **Find a way to mark or tag items you're considering letting go of.** Hang a tag with the date over the hanger of an article of clothing, or turn the hanger around to face the opposite direction of the other hangers. If you have not worn the item by the end of the season or within a certain time frame of the date on the tag, find it a new home. Use dated sticky notes to flag other items you think you're ready to let go of, and dispose of them if you don't use them by an expiration date of your choosing.

7. **Consider the seasonal separation.** Decorating for a holiday? Donate the decorations you don't use instead of putting them back in the box. Changing clothes from one season to the next? Don't let anything you felt less than fabulous in make the cut.

8. **Keep an open donation box** to make it easy to get things out of circulation as soon as you decide to part with them. When it's full, put it in

the trunk of your car or call someone to come pick it up. Feeling determined to let things go? Make a one-way rule for the box — things can go in, but they can't come back out.

Can't quite do all eight? That's okay. Consider these standards to aim for. Meanwhile, if you're able to stick to guidelines in most areas, one or two small exceptions won't be a big deal.

CHAPTER 8

E: Easy Upkeep

Therefore do not throw away your
confidence, which has a great reward.
HEBREWS 10:35

Easy upkeep. Sounds too good to be true, doesn't it? But everything you've been doing to this point has laid the foundation for just that.

Let's take a look at what you've done so far.

In the first three chapters, you identified the personal and organizational styles that will lay the foundation for your organizational systems.

In chapter 4, you started with successes, identifying the systems, containers, locations, and approaches that match your styles. Perhaps you even eliminated a few organizers or systems that weren't working, replaced them with something that's a better fit for your styles, or made plans to do so.

In chapter 5, you took small steps, zooming in on the value of making progress via baby steps. Perhaps you even tried out a few small steps of your own, tackling big problems a little bit at a time. Maybe you've even worked those baby steps into your routine.

In chapter 6, you analyzed the homes you'd assigned to your things, considering what the concept of location means for your belongings. Perhaps you even found new, logical, consistent homes for a few of them.

In chapter 7, you worked to let it go, considering the role downsizing plays in the overall process of organization, and giving some thought to where things you're finished with can go. Perhaps you even did some recycling and repurposing of your own.

All this brings us to Easy Upkeep, the last piece of the STYLE process. Easy Upkeep is all about finding what works and replicating it. This final step pulls together everything we've done so far — the successes, the organizational plans, the containers, the small steps, the new habits, and the new homes. Easy Upkeep includes troubleshooting and refining, replicating things that work, tossing out things that don't, and adjusting the things that sort of work. Bit by bit, we create a cohesive system that makes sense to us.

The end goal? A system that flows smoothly and requires minimal time and energy to maintain. Just because we've all landed in this chapter together, however, doesn't mean we're all at the same place in our process. Some of you are reading this thinking, "Troubleshoot? Refine? I've barely begun!" while others are nodding and saying, "Yes! Let's dig in!"

Wherever you are in the organization process, this chapter is for you. But before we move forward, let's take a moment to celebrate your accomplishments. Have you freed up space? Found new containers? Determined strategies that work for you? Located the perfect tool or container to solve a problem? All these things not only help to form the foundation of your organizational systems but lay the groundwork for the next steps as well.

Using the Planning for Easy Upkeep sheet on the next page, take a moment to assess where you are now and where you want to go. Answer the questions in the way that feels most true to you, even if that means repeating yourself and giving the same answer to more than one question.

Planning for Easy Upkeep

1. The most meaningful change I've made so far is ...

2. One new habit I've developed is ...

3. One discovery I've made about myself when it comes to organizing is ...

4. One organizational accomplishment I'm particularly proud of is ...

5. One thing I need to do to keep this all going is ...

6. Moving forward, one thing I want to remember is ...

Once you've answered these questions, **Easy Upkeep** becomes less mysterious. Your answers to items one through five — the changes you've made (#1), the habits you've developed (#2), the discoveries you've made (#3), your accomplishments so far (#4), and the momentum you've built (#5) — will create the action steps for your personalized version of **Easy Upkeep**. Together with your simple reminder (#6), these answers prepare you to replicate, refine, and create systems true to your styles.

Your most meaningful change (#1) becomes something you can generalize. If it's a change in your thought process (the way you look at organizing), you can use it to change the way you think through/plan out your organizational systems from now on. If it's a change in your approach (the way you tackle an organizational challenge), you can put that new approach to work every time you're confronted with an organizational challenge. If it's a change in a container, such as ditching an old standby for something that actually works for you, this change can lead you to explore a whole new set of tools. After all, if it worked in one place, it might work somewhere else, too.

Your new habit (#2) becomes just that — a new tactic in an old game where you emerge not only victorious but sustainably organized. As you come to understand the role this new habit plays and how it supports your styles, this habit, practiced regularly, can help you take positive steps forward as a regular part of your daily organizing.

I hope that **your discovery about yourself (#3)** has led you to a greater appreciation of yourself, your styles, and how you naturally approach organization. But even if this discovery is something you want to change (like putting things away instead of down), it can lead to new habits that support your styles. Though our styles might have been stumbling blocks in the past, each style has positive attributes as well. We can use those as a foundation, building on them as we create and sustain our organizational systems.

Your biggest accomplishment so far (#4) is the key to determining what you will replicate. Whether it's a discovery about something that works or about yourself, a habit, a container style, or a makeover of a former hot spot, what worked in one place will often work in another.

Your driving force (#5) can be a small step (**Don't put it down, put it away!**), a new habit (the one in #2 above or a different one), your simple reminder (#6 below), or something else entirely (appreciating the beauty of clear space). This driving force is what keeps this process moving forward — the thing that moves you toward using what you've set up, replicating what works, and troubleshooting what doesn't.

Easy Upkeep is, at its heart, the simplest of the steps — the one where we extend everything we've learned so far to new spaces and new challenges. Notice, though, that the "E" stands for "easy," not "effortless." **Your simple reminder (#6)** is the mantra you can fall back on when the upkeep feels anything but easy. It will nudge you forward, reminding you that what seems impossible is, indeed, possible.

My simple reminder? "It's a process."

Take a moment now to walk through your house and take note of areas where the upkeep is easy. You can simply make mental notes of which organizational systems are working well, or you can do this literally by making a list to keep track of your accomplishments. If you're more visual, you might take pictures of everything that's working.

If your house is like mine, you'll inevitably walk by some areas in need of troubleshooting, as well as what I call "hot spots" — consistent problem areas that seem to resist every intervention you've tried so far. We'll get to those in a moment, but for now take a moment to revel in your **Easy Upkeep** zones, and ask yourself a few questions:

- What do I like best about each of these areas?
- What do all these areas have in common?
- How can I replicate what I'm doing here in other areas of my home/workplace?

These are the keys to Easy Upkeep. When you're ready, armed

with these keys, let's move forward and troubleshoot.

•••

One staple in the troubleshooting toolbox is the STYLE process itself. Often, if the upkeep *isn't* easy, that's a sign that we should, perhaps, go back a few steps. Perhaps you have a hot spot or two in your home. A place where things get dumped. A place no container seems able to contain. If so, find (or imagine) that hot spot and let's use the STYLE process to troubleshoot.

When we **Start with successes**, we look at what we're doing well and use that to set up systems that use our styles as our guide for locations, containers, and systems. Are the containers and systems in this hot spot a good fit for the styles of everyone who uses the space? If not, can you replicate a system that's working elsewhere? Before you make any changes, though, pay attention to what *is* working with your current plan and make sure the new system will accomplish that as well.

When we **Take small steps**, we make progress a little at time and change things slowly instead of attempting a complete overhaul and trying to accomplish too much project in too little time. What's one small step you can take *right now* to restore order? Can you replace a container? Do some constructive sorting? **Give it five** to get a sense of the bones of the current system to see what's worth keeping and what's not?

When we embrace the idea that **Yes, it has a home**, the locations for our things make sense, based on both usage and our styles. Is everything in this hot spot in its home? Or, did this hot spot come to be because it's full of homeless items? If the items with homes were returned to their proper locations, would this hot spot disappear?

Acknowledging the importance of **Let it go!** as part of the process helps us to keep nonessential items out of the mix. Is there anything in this hot spot (including containers/organizers) you can let go of? Anything you can toss, recycle, repurpose, or relocate?

Finally, keeping your success zones in mind, ask yourself one last question about this hot spot: How can I make this easier?

Sometimes, in our enthusiasm for newer and better, we make things too complicated. Assess the hot spot with an eye toward simplifying. Is there an easier, style-friendly way to set up this space?

In the end, **Easy Upkeep** comes down to three things:

1. **Putting your systems to work.** If you've set things up based on your styles, easy upkeep should be a snap. And, even if the setup isn't perfect, it should work well enough that a few tweaks can take it from good to even better, simply by ...

2. **Adjusting where necessary.** A little trial and error can be an essential part of establishing a system that works. When you've got a strengths-based foundation, troubleshooting is easier because you can actually put your ideas to the test. Every time you adapt an existing system, it gets better *and* it informs future organizing.

3. **Valuing the clear space.** Once you've cleared a space, resist the urge to drop and run! You worked hard to create clear space, so you should enjoy the accomplishment.

Don't be discouraged if **Easy Upkeep** makes an appearance only in some areas at first. Once you get the knack of Organizing by STYLE, the upkeep gets easier because the more comfortable we become with our styles, the more readily solutions present themselves, and the better we get at taking what worked in one space and transferring those successes to other areas.

One final caveat: **Easy Upkeep** doesn't mean things will be perfect all the time. What it does mean is that you have a system in place that works for you, and when things begin to feel disorganized, you know what to do to set them right. And that can make things feel easy indeed.

KNOW THYSELF

As much as I know (and preach!) that organization is a process, I still hold out hope that there will actually come a day when everything in my house will be put away — and not haphazardly, but rather in a neat and logical fashion. From basement to crawlspace (and everything in between), my home will not only *look* tidy, but *be* tidy. Organizationally speaking, I will have arrived. There will be nothing left to sort, store, or systematize.

Clearly, my need for perfection, like my organization, is a work in progress.

But organization is as much about confidence as containers, and as much about peace of mind as perfection. When we're in control of our stuff instead of vice versa, we don't feel as though we're constantly trying to get ahead of this pile or that stack. When it's as easy to put things away as it is to put them down, fewer of our belongings lurk on flat surfaces, distracting us from the things that really matter: family, friends, and prayer.

Organization is a life skill, but it shouldn't consume our whole lives. Of all the reasons to get organized, perhaps the most important is a sense of mastery over our surroundings. Clear spaces yield peace of mind and a sense of relaxation, while logical homes that allow us to find what we need when we need it save us time and energy, freeing us to spend those valuable, finite commodities on the things that really matter.

Why do you want to be organized? When will you know you have arrived?

Smart organizers know when to ask for help.
Dear Lord, thank you for the progress I have made. Help me to appreciate my own uniqueness and the uniqueness of each member of my family as we move forward together in this journey. Amen.

LISA'S LISTS

Three Foundations of Easy Upkeep

Easy upkeep is what we're all aiming for. Can you love, honor, and cherish its foundations?

1. **Honor your styles.** You've defined them. You've come to terms with them (or made progress in that direction anyway). Maybe you've even developed a sense of humor about them. Regardless of where you are on the "I love my styles!" continuum, you've discovered the default settings that underlie how you think and how you organize. Respect these and let them lead the way to containers, setups, and systems that feel right to you, regardless of what someone with different styles might think — or say.

2. **Honor your systems.** Your systems consist of the homes you've established for your things and the containers (from the smallest subdivision of a drawer to the largest room in your house) you've selected to house them. If you've honored your styles in the space you have, the resulting systems will eventually flow naturally from what you automatically do. Will you find the perfect container and the perfect spot immediately for every single thing? Nope. That's where the refining and troubleshooting come in.

3. **Honor your choices**, but remember that not everyone's choices are the same. The whole concept of Organizing by STYLE is built around the

idea that when it comes to organizing, one size does *not* fit all. You may love using a certain type of container or storage system, but that doesn't mean that everyone else in your house will appreciate it (let alone use it) as well. If your house is like my house, numerous styles prevail ... and collide. If you have any hope of the upkeep being easy, you need to find the sweet spot between your styles and the styles of those who live with you.

PART III

Living in STYLE

CHAPTER 9

Organizing Obstacles

*Consider it all joy, my brethren, when you
meet various trials, for you know that the
testing of your faith produces steadfastness.*
JAMES 1:2–3

No matter how well-organized we are, there are times when we just can't keep up. Clutter invades clear spaces. Things get put down instead of put away. Our containers and systems can't keep up, and neither can we.

When this happens, remember that you haven't failed and this is *not* the time to throw in the towel. Instead, it's time to reassess and return to what works — containers based on your styles, locations that make sense, and systems that combine knowledge with practice.

But different challenges call for different solutions, so let's take them one at a time.

NOT ENOUGH TIME

The problem: Everything was working until I got busy. Now it feels like I'm starting over!

The solution: Start with successes and use small pockets of time to restore order.

Instead of looking at busy times as an indication that everything is falling apart, think of busy times as an opportunity to take stock. When you finally manage to eke out a few minutes to restore order, what can be put away quickly and easily? That's a sign of a working system. The containers and systems that work even when time is scarce will be your ports in the storm. These are the things you want to replicate in other areas where successes are less apparent.

On the other hand, what do you end up holding in your hand, trying to find a place for? What do you set down beside the container it's supposed to go into instead of putting it inside?

Stop for a moment and take a look at *why* you're stymied by that homeless item or stopping inches short of its destination. Is the container too small? Too complicated? Overstuffed? Is the location illogical? What would make it easy for you to put that item exactly where it belongs?

Once you've determined what's keeping your containers and systems from working, go back to your styles. Shun the "shoulds" in favor of containers that work for the person using the system. That means saying "Thanks, but no thanks" to your husband's insistent suggestion that a file cabinet would be the "perfect" solution (unless he's doing the filing) and going with the container that matches your daughter's style for organizing her tasks. And if you're in charge of that particular put-away? You call the shots.

Finally, shift your focus so that you zoom in on what you've accomplished. So often, we completely discount what we've accomplished and magnify what remains undone. Sure, there's still stuff to do and to put away. Until things slow down a bit, concentrate on using small pockets of time to make a dent in the detritus (**Give it five!**) and then congratulate yourself for the progress you make instead of beating up on yourself for not getting every last thing done.

My favorite fast fix: fabric bins on shelves under my mail counter to collect catalogs. It takes less than a minute to sort the catalogs, drop the keepers into the bin, and recycle the rest. Then, when the bin is full, it's time to go through it and toss duplicates and anything past its prime.

NOT ENOUGH SPACE

The problem: Ugh! If only I had one more closet! Or maybe an extra room …

The solution: Style-based strategies and a little out-of-the-box thinking.

If I had a nickel for every time I wished for an extra room or a bigger house, I'd have a down payment on a house with multiple walk-in closets.

Sure, an extra room, or even an extra closet might be a game changer. So, if it's within your means and you have the space, why not build or buy one? Be careful, though — extra space can be a lifesaver, or it can be a magnet for clutter. Smaller spaces force us to be more efficient simply because there's no room for extraneous stuff.

The first step to resolving the "not enough space" problem is to make sure we really need all the stuff that's in the space. Are there things you can donate or dispose of, or is everything worth keeping? If you suspect that the space crunch has as much to do with too much stuff as not enough space, flip back to chapter 7 for some ways to manage the downsizing dilemma.

If everything in your too-small space is a keeper, it's time to consider how well you're using the space. Do your furniture pieces serve more than one purpose? Storage benches and ottomans give us places to sit and prop our feet but also hide games, toys, and outside equipment. Coffee tables and media units that don't also provide storage may be taking up more than their fair share of space. Subdividing drawers, shelves, and closets can maximize space as well.

Moving beyond the traditional use of things can also help. Just because a manufacturer labels an item one thing doesn't mean you can't use it for something else. Consider your styles and how much space you have, then look for a piece that fits. Putting your styles ahead of the item's designated function gives you the freedom to get creative and come up with unique solutions that work for you.

My favorite space saver: Our family room is actually a downstairs bedroom. Instead of a media center, we put our television on the top shelf of an open storage unit that holds fabric cubes. The unit was very inexpensive, and the cubes and bins hold (and hide) files, reading material, and fleece blankets.

IT'S JUST NOT WORKING

The problem: I thought I had this all figured out, but my "perfect system" is falling apart!

The solution: Back to basics

The foundation of Organizing by STYLE is habit — factoring the things we do automatically into our organizational systems so they feel natural and work as effortlessly as possible. But the path to the perfect solution can be full of detours. We get sucked in by the hype (this will solve all your organizational problems!), the look (so pretty!), the price (It's on sale! Or, I already have this, so I might as well use it instead of buying something else), or someone else's style (all you need is a file cabinet and a couple of binders).

And then we wonder why it's not working.

Even without these detours, though, the path can be bumpy. We get all excited and choose a container that we think will work, or we set up a system that we're sure will be a time-saver, and it just doesn't live up to its promise.

The good news is that every imperfect solution gives us clues to one that's better. When your perfect system is just not working, the next step is as close as a single question.

Why?

Is it not big enough? too out of the way? just too much trouble?

If these questions sound familiar, congratulations! (And thanks for paying attention!) I raised them (or some just like them) a few pages ago when we were dealing with the "not enough time" conundrum.

There's nothing like a time crunch to point out what's not working, which can quickly send us down the "nothing's working!" rabbit hole. Typically, however, something is working. And, when we remove the time crunch, we can quickly go back through the STYLE process to troubleshoot:

Start with successes: *What is working?*
Take small steps: *Can I make one small change, or do I need to start over?*
Yes, it has a home: *Does everything that's here belong here?*
Let it go!: *If I remove what doesn't belong, will I solve the problem? Or do I need to let this container go and find a new one?*
Easy upkeep: *What's the next step toward making this work better?*

Once you've answered these questions, you're on your way to a new approach — one that replicates the successes of your existing system while removing the obstacles. The next thing you try might solve the problem, or you might need a few more attempts to get it just right. Then, once it's just right, you can chalk it up as a success whether you're functioning as Wendy (or Wally) Whirlwind or a lady (or gentleman) of leisure.

Sometimes, though, it's not just the tools that need to be changed. Perhaps the system is just fine and it's our habits that need to be adjusted. In our family room, we have a gray bin with a lid that lifts up. Because I often work in our family room, this wonderful gray bin (chosen after much deliberation with a precise purpose in mind) exists entirely to hide my projects-in-progress. It's roomy, easily accessible (just lift the lid and drop the item in), a fit for my *drop and run* organizational style, and just steps away from the sofa where I sit with my laptop.

It's the perfect tool.

Yet some nights, I set things down on the table *beside the bin.*

This is not the fault of the bin. This is operator error.

Sometimes, our habits are building blocks. Other times, they are stumbling blocks. The trick to troubleshooting is being honest with ourselves about what we need to do to take a container or system from not working to working.

My favorite makeover: Besides my gray bin? My mail counter.

Once a towering pile of catalogs and stuff to sort, it is now under control (most of the time) thanks to a combination of bins for catalogs, an open-top file holder and a now-established habit of sorting through the mail when I bring it into the house. Most days, anyway.

WARRING STYLES

The problem: I've got my stuff figured out, but *their* stuff is everywhere!
The solution: Educate, evaluate, and compromise.

You've taken the quiz. You've identified your styles. You've figured out what works for you, and you're proud of the progress you've made.

But your family members are grumbling. The systems you love are the systems they love to hate. Or perhaps the reverse is true. They say they've got it all figured out, but it certainly doesn't look that way to you.

The first step here is figuring out who uses the system the most. If you're the one in charge of organizing the space in question, the containers and systems should be based on *your* styles. But before you get too excited, keep in mind that the reverse is true as well. If it's your spouse or children who are in charge of the space, *their* styles should prevail.

Either way, understanding each other's styles is important not only to keeping a tidy living space, but also to keeping the peace. Share the "why" behind your organizational choices with your family and listen to your family members' reasons for their selections. Together, decide which systems, particularly in shared living spaces, are being used consistently and effectively and which are less than ideal.

For systems/containers that aren't working (that is, no one is actually using them and/or an organizational issue is apparent), try to find the points of agreement between styles before settling on a new solution. Clear or labeled containers, for example, can work for both the *I need to see it* and the *I know I put it somewhere* organizational styles, albeit for different reasons.

If the systems/containers *are* working, you probably didn't need to have this discussion in the first place. Practice a little patience and, in non-shared spaces, close the door, walk away, or otherwise put some distance between yourself and the alleged problem — unless you want to take over maintenance of the space in question.

We'll talk more about organizing with kids in chapter 10.

My favorite perspective check: Not my circus, not my monkey.

SEASONS (OF THE YEAR AND OF LIFE)

The problem: I know I should be enjoying this season, but I'm too tired to be enthusiastic.

The solution: Zoom in on what matters and take small steps toward the rest.

Raise your hand if you used to love _____ (fill in the blank: Christmas, Thanksgiving, Mother's Day, etc.), but now it just sounds exhausting.

Fa la la la la, indeed.

At our house we store Christmas decorations in the crawl-space, though as our collection has grown, some are in the basement. The older I get, the harder it is to access these treasures. I don't bend and lug and pull with the same ease or grace I did in my thirties when there was a lot less stuff in the crawlspace. I'm not happy about this, but it's not something that's likely to change unless I miraculously become more spry and/or I clear a *lot* of stuff out of that space.

One year, when my daughter was small, I took stock of the

situation and decided the problem wasn't just me. The containers were all wrong. I couldn't see what was in them until I pulled them out, and most contained both things I loved and things that might never come out again. Because it was a pain to take the oversized bins out in the first place, once they were out, they sat half full in the living space until after the holidays.

Unwieldy. Unacceptable. And annoying.

I decided that the red and green bins I'd had to have after Christmas a few years before had been a bad decision. What I really needed was something that let me see what was in the containers before I pulled them out, or better yet, a container I didn't have to pull out at all.

After Christmas that year, we replaced the big red and green tubs with two clear-plastic three-drawer units. Thanks to a simple change in containers, I no longer lug overstuffed bins out of the crawlspace. Now, I open a drawer, pull out what I want and take only those items out. This allows me to decorate in stages (all the things I like to put out first are in one of two drawers), which is essential since final exams and decorating for Christmas collide every year. In addition, I procrastinate less (notice I didn't say "not at all"). I still have to stoop — it is a crawlspace, after all — but I don't have to lug.

Once I'd put the system to work and it had proven its value, I expanded it to include drawers for other holidays for which I have decorations.

Wow — what a difference! The process was easier, I was happier, and the house was (a little) less cluttered.

What, you may ask, is the point of this story?

Sometimes we need to use a system for a while before we know what's wrong with it. Because we access holiday things only once a year, we sometimes use the same system for a very long time, even when we've outgrown it, or it no longer meets our needs. In addition, when it comes to holidays, many of us vow every year to simplify and promise ourselves that "next year, I'll ... " But we get busy, so we keep using a broken system because it's easier than starting over, and so, the next year, we're in the same rut again.

The time to consider these changes is before next year arrives. Troubleshooting my organizational system before the holidays allowed me to figure out what I needed to do differently. By creating my "next year" wish list this year, I was able to jump-start what I wanted to do differently *and* take advantage of after-holiday sales to do it more cheaply.

If your holiday organization isn't working for you, troubleshoot as you go. For example, as you take the decorations out, consider what's wrong with the way the decorations are stored. What would make the system easier, more accessible, more streamlined — whatever it is that you think you need to change? Change it before it's time to put things away again.

Other times, our holiday exhaustion is less of an organizational issue than an issue of priorities. In our well-intentioned desire to create the best holiday ever, we end up with a beautifully decorated house; fabulous, well-prepared meals; and the most important things on everyone's wish list — only to be too exhausted to enjoy them. Or we create unrealistic lists and expectations, and when we have to eliminate items, we feel as though we've failed.

We don't have to do it all.

I'm going to say that again. We don't have to do it all.

Having a wonderful holiday is about deciding what matters most and putting those things at the top of the list. Then, if you don't get to everything, you'll know you've at least done the things that have the most meaning.

Together with your family, decide ahead of time what the most important aspects of the holiday are. You can begin with a simple question over dinner like, "What's everyone looking forward to this Christmas?" Or you can make it a guessing game. Have each family member try to guess another family member's favorite holiday tradition. These conversations will help you tease out what's most important to the people you celebrate with, alleviating any guilt you might feel about cutting back. Maybe even go a step further and see what nonmaterial thing everyone has always thought might be a fun part of the holidays. Once again, I repeat: We don't have to do it all.

Chances are, something that's on your to-do list is missing from theirs — and, I must say, in the spirit of full disclosure, vice versa. Did anyone ask for a ten-course feast, or did one of your kids suggest that pizza for Christmas Eve dinner — or even Thanksgiving — sounded like fun? Are there traditions that make it to that overwhelming holiday to-do list only because that's the way you've always done things?

Depending on the composition of your family (mostly adults? mostly kids? nuclear, blended, or extended?), you can take the direct approach. Let your family know that you'd like to simplify the holiday frenzy and ask them if there are traditions they'd prefer to set aside. Chances are, some of them have asked, "Do we *have* to do this?" about at least one part of the alleged festivities on at least one occasion, and they might be even more excited than you are about crossing it off the list. Or keep it even simpler. Ask each family member to make a list of their top three holiday traditions. Combine the lists and see if, together, they create the basics of your family's holiday to-do list.

At the risk of sounding like a broken record, let me repeat that. *Your* family's to-do list. The one that's customized for what matters to the unique individuals who make up *your* family.

Perhaps, in the end, you'll opt to keep everything and celebrate the holidays in exactly the same way you always have — but at least you'll have *chosen* to do so. **Let it go!** can be just as challenging for traditions as it is for belongings, but in both cases a thoughtful approach can make the difference between being satisfied with what we keep and being overwhelmed by it.

And it's not just the actual holidays — it's also seasons of life. When our kids are little, the whirlwind swirls almost continuously, and we're so busy doing what we have to do that we have little time to consider what we want to do. As they (and we) grow older, it becomes easier to take a step back and ask ourselves "What really matters here?"

As I write this, it is Saturday afternoon, and my young adult daughter is home for the weekend. My dad, now a widower, lives about seven minutes away. My husband, an early riser, is chomping at the bit to do something as my daughter naps, and I alternate between writing and doing laundry. I want

- to finish this chapter and keep writing;
- to spend time with my family while all of us are under the same roof; and
- to make sure that my daughter and my father get some time together before she boards another train tomorrow afternoon.

If I keep writing after I finish this chapter, the other two things won't happen, so clearly I have to revise item #1 to make #2 and #3 possible. While I know this on many levels, it doesn't make stepping away from my laptop when I'm on a roll any easier, but since the writing isn't priority #1 today, I might just have to set it aside.

Finally, sometimes we have no idea how we're going to make it all happen. We make lists, and we get stymied by real life, running up against obstacle after obstacle. We can try to power through, like a runner jumping hurdles; or we can decide that, in those times especially, we have to trust that God knows what our schedules should look like even better than we do.

And, if we choose that second option, we can trust that we're exactly where we're supposed to be, even if it isn't where we planned to be.

My favorite holiday mantras: (1) one thing at a time, and (2) God is in charge of my day.

MOTIVATION (OR THE LACK THEREOF)

The problem: I just don't wanna.
The solution: Then don't.

Really.

For better or for worse, it'll all be there tomorrow. For today, here's what not to do. Do not beat yourself up. Do not call yourself lazy or rebuke yourself in any way. If you're truly tired, curl up under a cozy blanket and take a nap (if you can), because that's the best organization strategy there is when you're too tired to think. Then, once you're rested, dig in.

You're not that kind of tired, you say? You are tired of clutter, tired of picking up after everyone else, tired of it all being so much *work*?

Ah. *That* tired.

How about this: Can you make it better? Just a little bit better? Can you start somewhere, anywhere, and make a dent, even if it's one only you will notice?

A few years ago, I spent part of several mornings revamping two drawers in my dining room. I emptied them out, lined them, and then subdivided the space using plastic drawer organizers. One became a drawer for the company "silverware" (stainless steel — silver is lovely but much too much work), and the other became a utility drawer of sorts, creating a home for a variety of items that always got tossed "somewhere" — wherever there was space, and often not the same space twice. After my drawer intervention, each of those items had its own spot in a neatly subdivided drawer.

No one else noticed, but I didn't care. To this day, I smile when I open them. They're beautifully organized, in true *I need to see it/drop and run* style.

My favorite nudge to action: When you feel overwhelmed, ask yourself this: "What one thing would give me the biggest sense of accomplishment right now?"

THAT PROCRASTINATION SENSATION

The problem: This all sounds great. I'll do it tomorrow.
The solution: Take small steps.

I could write an entire book on procrastination, and half of it would be about the creative ways I've found to make everything a priority except the thing I should be doing. In fact, one of the reasons I sometimes need to leave my house and go somewhere else to write is that if I stay at home, I can find too many other things to do instead. Laundry never looked more interesting. Unloading the dishwasher never seemed so important. And that stack of papers that's been collecting dust on the dining room table for an unspecified length of time? I'm suddenly overwhelmed by the urgency to file those papers *right now*.

We procrastinate for a variety of reasons. Two of the most common are feeling overwhelmed by what needs to be done and pressuring ourselves to do it perfectly.

Let's get that second one out of the way right now. It's not going to be perfect. Organization is a process, a constant work in progress. This can be exhausting or exhilarating, depending on your outlook, but it's unavoidable. Why? Because part of the nature of life is that "stuff" comes and goes. We can control the flow to a certain extent, but we can't stop it entirely. There will always be something to put away, replace, or get rid of. The better our systems get, the more quickly and easily this can happen, but sometimes we outgrow our once-perfect systems or simply find a better solution.

So. What to do? Settle for the imperfect — intentionally. For now, choose a tool you have on hand or a not-quite-right location as a temporary placeholder. Use it. Complain about all the ways it doesn't work. Figure out why it's so incredibly subpar. Before you know it, you'll know exactly what you need to do. And then? Wait for it. You might just get your perfect solution after all.

My favorite procrastination busters are a process step and a strategy: **Take small steps** and **Give it five!**

BUT YOU DON'T UNDERSTAND. I'M. JUST. TOTALLY. OVERWHELMED.

I get it. So, here's what you do. Start somewhere. Anywhere. Pick up that piece of paper in front of you, the remote control someone left on the sofa, the stack of folders you've been meaning to file. Wherever you decide to start is the right place to start as long as it gets you moving, because the secret to organizing, as with so many other things, is to just *start*. For some inexplicable reason the first step is a mile long and then, miraculously, the ones that follow become more manageable. Often, by starting with the small things — the things that are right in front of us, the ones that didn't even make it onto the to-do list yet — we gain both the momentum and the courage to tackle the ones that seem insurmountable.

It would be wonderful if we could get to Easy Upkeep and achieve organizational perfection, but life is meant to move forward. As it does, our systems need to adapt to the changes. Whether you're adding to your family, downsizing, or just trying to keep up with the day-to-day, your organizational systems need to be dynamic, adjusting to the lives they're meant to keep in order. Once we accept that "perfectly organized" is an ephemeral state at best, *that's* when the upkeep finally gets easy.

Most days, anyway.

KNOW THYSELF

Have you ever had one of those days where you hit the ground running, visions of productivity dancing like sugar plums in your head, but end up having to clear hurdle after hurdle on the way to the finish line? You've made your list, you've planned it all out — you've gotten organized! — but you are thwarted at every turn.

Of course you have. Welcome to life as we know it.

Making plans isn't a bad thing, but we need to remember that there's a larger plan at work, and it's not one of our own design. I know that God has an enduring plan for me, one that promises me not harm, but hope, but I sometimes (okay, often) lose sight of this in the crush of everyday to-do lists. Worse yet, I mistakenly feel a responsibility to be large and in charge all on my own and forget that I have a rock I can lean on.

Strangely enough (but not by accident, I'm sure), I often encounter pleasant surprises on those days where things stray far from my plan — encounters that remind me of the bigger picture. I leave the house much later than expected only to run into an old friend at my destination — one who wouldn't have been in that same place had I arrived when I'd intended. I spend more time — or less — on a task only to discover that I finish it just in time to do something else that wasn't on the schedule. I share a story I hadn't intended to share only to discover that the person I'm telling is exactly the person who can help me — or a person who needed that story at that very moment.

When we stumble over life's inevitable obstacles, perhaps we need to reframe them as detours. Yes, we've taken a path that is different from the one our internal GPS has recommended, but it's possible that the road we've ended up on has more to offer. Perhaps it's more scenic, offering us an unexpected opportunity to slow down; or, perhaps it gets us to a place just north or south of our intended destination — which turns out to be an even better spot.

Organization is a process, and so is life. We learn as we go, honing our skills and zooming in on the things that really matter. How can you reframe your organizational obstacles as detours? Might these side trips benefit you in the long run?

Smart organizers know when to ask for help. *Dear Lord, thank you for bringing me this far in my organizational journey. Help me to remember that I don't have to be perfect, I just have to be me. Amen.*

LISA'S LISTS

Ten Things You Can Do in Ten Minutes (or Less)

Every baby step forward is a step in the right direction.

How can you use just ten minutes to your organizational advantage?

1. Unload the dishwasher.

2. Sort the mail.

3. Thin out your catalog collection by eliminating duplicates.

4. Fold a load of laundry.

5. Tidy one drawer or shelf.

6. Put ten things where they belong.

7. Corral all the clutter from one room into a container (a laundry basket or bin, for example).

8. Shorten a stack of papers by starting from the bottom and putting things where they belong.

9. Assess why a container isn't earning its keep.

10. Create a to-do list.

CHAPTER 10

Organizing with Kids

*For God did not give us a
spirit of timidity but rather of
power and love and self-control.*
2 TIMOTHY 1:7

Organizing with kids can be a blast. Or it can be a nightmare. They can bring enthusiasm and great ideas to the process, or they can dig their heels in and pout.

Y'know. Kind of like … us?

All kidding aside, organizing can be a big job for a little person. It's not nearly as much fun as watching television, reading a good book, or playing with friends. In addition, kids who struggle with organization feel a lot like adults who are organizational works-in-progress. Embarrassed. Self-conscious. Wondering why the rest of the world "gets it" and they don't.

Kids younger than preschool aren't quite ready to take on organizing by themselves, leaving you to lead the way. Primary school kiddos will still need an assist. They'll get, as we used to say when my daughter was little, "an opinion, not a vote." Together, you can identify their styles and gather their input, but you'll still be leading. Upper-elementary-aged children are old enough to introduce to Organizing by STYLE; in fact, my first Organizing by STYLE small group was with third-graders, and every fall, I did a unit on the topic in all my fifth-grade classes.

Do you have a child you think is old enough to introduce to Organizing by STYLE?

Let's go!

Together with your child, flip back to chapter 1. Describe the characters in the first chapter, or, if your child is old enough, have him (or her) read the chapter independently, with the goal of finding things that are "like him" (or her) in Gemma and her kids. Beginning the process by identifying with someone else, like a fictional character in a novel, can make kids feel less self-conscious and can spark a conversation — and maybe even a little motivation.

Then take the Styles Quiz with your kids. Yes, I know you've already taken it, but, in the spirit of solidarity and relationship-building, give it another shot. While helping kids identify their default settings is the key to understanding what will work for them and what won't, having a partner in this battle is a confidence-builder. If we don't build our children's confidence in their organizational skills, along with the skills themselves, we may win the battle but lose the war. Getting comfortable with who we are and how we work is as important to Organizing by STYLE as any tool or technique; owning our styles is the key to choosing containers and creating systems that work for us. Once you've finished with chapter 1 and the Styles Quiz, take some time to chat with your child. Begin by asking him to identify the things he's doing that work. If he's stumped, help him out. What always (or at least most of the time) gets put away? What can she always (or at least most of the time) find? Remember, we're not looking for perfection here — just consistency and successes we can build on.

Finally, go to a spot over which he has ownership and **Give it five!** Set a timer for five minutes and spend five minutes in the space. *How* you and your child spend the five minutes is up to your child. You can list everything that's working. You can troubleshoot the things that aren't. You can dream up new solutions for hot spots. You can identify containers that are overworked, overflowing, or totally empty. You can have a race to see who picks up and puts away the most stuff before the timer goes off. The goal here is to leave your child feeling as though he or she is in charge and has taken a step forward. Beyond that, the only nonnegotiable is that when the timer goes off, you're finished. Prepare yourself to watch your child go bounding off to something more fun the second that timer rings. Don't worry. Rest assured that you've planted seeds you can harvest later. And if she goes bounding off, your job is to follow. No fair staying behind to do one more thing.

Zoom out. Big picture. You want to get your child on board and keep her there.

What if, miracle of miracles, your child wants to continue?

Resist the urge to do your happy dance and promise her a spending spree at the store of her choice or bake her a batch of chocolate chip cookies that she doesn't have to share with anyone. Simply ask if she wants your help, or if you should go. And then do what she requests. Let her know where you'll be if she needs you.

How your child feels at this point is the key to creating a positive path forward. When you walk out of that room, whether your child is ahead of you, beside you, or behind you continuing what the two of you started, you want him to feel as though you understand and respect his styles and that you're willing to give him a chance to do this on his terms.

Remember how liberating it felt when you took advantage of the same option?

Your confidence in him is the first step in his journey to confidence in himself. Today's task (the first step in that journey) centered on planting the seeds of a new way of thinking. From here, you can walk beside your child as he discovers his styles and puts them to work. Here are a few things he'll need from you.

OWNERSHIP

Once we've identified our children's styles, we might think we have the perfect tools, containers, or answers for them, but only they know if they'll really *use* the tools we offer. And if they won't use them, we'll only end up back where we started ... and a little poorer. Instead, help your children figure out their styles and be in charge of choosing the containers that they think will work for them. Although you might have already decided where they fit and what containers they need, if you let them tell you, you'll get a window into their thinking that will be helpful as you work together to strategize. As you work together, offer suggestions, but let them have the final say. I can promise you it *won't* work every time, but getting organized is a learning process. We sometimes learn as much from what doesn't work as we do from what does, and quite often we learn a lot from one another.

What about shared spaces such as kids' bedrooms? How do we organize when multiple styles are at work? This gets a little trickier but, whenever possible, let the style of the person who uses the system the most prevail. Two kids in the same bedroom should each choose the tools they use for their own things and should each get a say in shared spaces (like the closet). In family spaces, choosing containers that match your kids' styles can be a stepping-stone to handing over the responsibility of keeping the space tidy. Be clear on this from the outset, though. No fair berating them later to the tune of, "I chose this tool because you wanted it. Now you need to keep this room clean!"

Tempting, I know. It's a process — *especially* with kids.

ENCOURAGEMENT

Being your child's organizational cheerleader can be easy (and even fun) when you and your child share a personal and/or organizational style, but it becomes more challenging when your child's style is different and his systems are perhaps not yet established. Try not to judge. Kids know that cramming papers into a small space, collecting every rock and crayon, or dropping their shoes in the middle of the floor isn't the ideal organizational system. Gently redirect, if you can, and figure out homes and systems that work for both of you. Ask your child where he or she would put things ... or, if possible, place a style-appropriate container in the spot where he or she naturally drops stuff. Notice when something gets put where it belongs, returns home uncrushed and unfolded, or can be found when it's needed.

You don't have to throw a party. A smile will do. Maybe even an acknowledgment or a hug, if that works for both of you. Strategies like **Give it five!** build encouragement right in. When the timer goes off, you can both celebrate what was accomplished. Resist the temptation to point out how much still needs to be done, but if your child points it out, offer him the opportunity to reset the timer. Alternatively, if the amount of work that remains is stressing you out, suggest another time later in the day to **Give it five!** again.

Okay, okay, you're saying. This is all well and good when there are only a few things to pick up and put away. But what about those times when the space is so far gone that **Give it five!** feels like a drop of water in the ocean?

Divide and conquer. If it's a bedroom or another area that's not public space (i.e., anyone coming into your home can see it), choose a place to dig in. It might be the area that's most far gone, the area that can be resolved most easily, or the area for which your child has a style-specific solution in mind. Work together until that area looks better, then choose a time to tackle the next area.

Then shut the door and walk away.

While shared family spaces can get out of control, most of the time these are the areas we police the most, keeping them from crossing the line from manageable to unmanageable. Having each person come in and put his or her stuff where it belongs often suffices to jump-start the process. Once your kids are thinking in terms of styles, ask them to consider what would make this process easier for them. Their answers may range from choosing different homes or containers to changing their own habits. Try to keep an open mind.

And if the answer is, "If you did it for me," simply smile and acknowledge how nice it would be to have help. Then ask them what their Plan B is. Mom or Dad organizing their lives for them is not a sustainable or healthy plan for anyone above the age of four. If they can take it out, they can put it away.

A BUDGET

Identifying styles does not give us license to break the bank on custom containers and systems. This is a process, and a fluid one at that, replete with trial and error. Encourage your kids to start with dollar bins, dollar stores, clearance racks, and things you have on hand (not necessarily in that order). Once an item works (that is, it is used consistently and/or successfully solves an organizational challenge), an upgrade might make sense; until then, go cheap. Kids with a creative bent are often just as happy coming up with their own solutions (maybe even repurposing something you already have on hand) and personalizing them. Cardboard boxes trimmed to size and decorated with Washi tape or contact paper often make great (cheap) solutions. I built an entire filing system in my office out of decorative gift boxes I got on sale after Christmas.

TRICKS OF THE TRADE

Organization doesn't have to be an exhausting, weekend-erasing proposition. Introduce your kids to tools like **Give it five!** to make a dent in the piles and **Don't put it down, put it away!** to prevent clutter in the first place. Start small, involving your child in tasks where success is easy to see — a backpack, a drawer, a bookshelf — and work from there. Help them understand the importance of choosing locations that make sense, and containers that earn their keep by being both attractive and easy to use. Teach them the STYLE process, and the importance of starting with successes. Most of all, teach them to embrace their styles as a part of who they are, and to understand that organizing is something we all have to keep after and work at.

One last thing. Remember that the goal is to teach your child to have the confidence to organize independently. Once you've put your child in charge, *don't* go back and redo what he or she has done. Nothing wrecks confidence faster, not to mention inspires a complete lack of cooperation the next time around. For your sake as well as your child's, assist when asked, then walk away. Keeping your relationship with your child intact is more important than a tidy room.

BACK-TO-SCHOOL HELP

In chapter 9, we talked about seasons of the year (and of life) that impact us as adults. One of the seasons that impacts our kids at least as much as it impacts us is back-to-school time. For kids who are Type A organizers (yes, they exist), shopping is simple. Buy whatever the teacher puts on the list, secure in the knowledge that our naturally organized kids will use all of it successfully and as intended.

If you're having a teeny tiny pity party over the fact that the kids who live in your house aren't Type A organizers, stop. Yes, stop. And put it in reverse.

If you feel bad that your kids don't compare to those Type A organizers, imagine how your kids feel sitting in class all year long with kids who appear to organize effortlessly. Can you identify?

Back-to-school shopping is rife with challenges: adhering to the expectations of your child's school; finding the tools that are right for your child; managing wants, needs, and style-based selections on a budget.

While I would not recommend second-guessing a teacher's specific supply list, I am suspicious of the one-size-fits-all lists that stores make available. I always wonder who creates those lists, and whether everything on them is necessary, negotiable, or useful to every child. Take three-ring binders, for example. I hate them. Okay, I don't always hate them, but they definitely don't make my Most Valuable Tools list — though they're on the MVT list of almost every Type A organizer I've ever met.

Here's why binders and I don't get along. First, if the paper you're handing me is not prepunched with the right number of holes in the right spots for the binder I own, I already have a barrier to getting it from my hand into my storage system.

But let's say it's prepunched. Now what do I do with it? I open my binder. I flip through the sections. I locate the appropriate section. I figure out where the paper should go in that section. I open the rings. I put the paper inside. I close the rings. I close the binder.

Zzzzzzz.

No, that wasn't a typo. I must admit that, for the Type A organizer, all those (many) steps make perfect sense.

But what if your organizational style is *cram and jam*? That's an awful lot of trouble to go through, making it unlikely that those with a *cram and jam* organizational style will ever get that paper where it's supposed to go. Are they lazy? I would argue that they're not, but I'm sure there are those who would argue the opposite. But honestly, does it matter who's right?

That paper is not getting where it's supposed to go.

Those with an *I need to see it* personal style might actually go through all the steps (maybe), but once the binder is closed, the paper disappears. Out of sight, out of mind.

Kids with an *I know I put it somewhere* organizational style are likely to get it into the binder — somewhere — but have trouble retrieving it later because they just put it "somewhere." Maybe it's in the right section, maybe it isn't.

You may love binders. Your kids may love binders. If that's the case — hooray! One big, fat, hairy school-organization problem solved. Even though I don't typically find three-ring binders to be a good fit for my style, I readily admit that they work well for many people. Every tool has value, but not to every person. But every *child* has value, and making a child feel broken (or lazy) because the tool doesn't work with his or her style is not only hurtful, it's counterproductive.

Why not pick the right tool in the first place? That, my friends, is Plan A.

So where do you start? By making not just a supply list, but also a style list before you shop. Together with your child, use the Back-to-School Planning sheet on the next page to shape your shopping. Having your kids talk through the choices is an important part of getting them to understand their styles, and eventually, to advocate for themselves. When we teach our kids to respectfully advocate for themselves, we're teaching a skill that goes far beyond organization. Until they get there, however, going to bat for them is our job.

Back-to-School Planning

What are your styles?

Personal style:

Organizational style:

What worked last year?

What did *not* work last year?

What do you like?

I like organizers that are (circle all that apply):

see-through	color-coded	unusual
sectioned	by subject	fun to use
brightly colored	unique	other:

What's the hardest thing about staying organized at school?

Is there any particular organizer you'd like to try? If so, why?

Planners: Love them or hate them?

Remember:

- Choose containers that fit your styles.
- Match the size of the container to what it will store, with a little room to grow.
- Never underestimate the importance of a fun-to-use organizer.

●●●

How conclusive was your discussion? Don't despair if you didn't nail everything down. Chances are you learned *something* about what works for your child and what doesn't, and that information can guide your shopping and make it more strategic. Though the choices seem endless, it really all comes down to three basic things: a home for papers that need to be referenced, a home for papers that need to travel between point A (school) and point B (home), and a container to hold all the miscellany — pencils, erasers, highlighters, and so on. Elementary school students may be able to get away with one or two items for each of these categories, while middle and high school students will likely need to plan for each subject.

Let's take these one at a time.

A HOME FOR PAPERS TO REFERENCE

Items that go into this home range from content-related packets and class notes to cafeteria menus. For many kids (and most teachers), the container of choice for this job is a three-ring binder, but this isn't the best tool for every student. Those who aren't fans of the binder can try an accordion folder (or one for each subject, for older kids), a skinny binder with a clamp closure (or one for each subject, for older kids), a collection of folders color-coded by subject, or any other paper-holding container. Whatever it is, it needs to be durable and expandable so it can house everything from a single sheet of paper to multiple packets that cover entire units of study. In addition, this tool needs to fit into your child's allotted space at school (desk, cubby, locker, etc.). In fact, that's where these tools should live unless they're coming home explicitly so your child can study for a test.

Many teachers require binders, so before you purchase something that's not on the list of required items, check to make sure your child will be allowed to use it. If the answer is no, see Lisa's Lists at the end of this chapter for ideas on upgrading that required binder to make it a bit more style-friendly.

A HOME FOR PAPERS TO DEAL WITH

Items in this category include homework, permission slips, and flyers announcing school events. The container of choice for this job will function as a holding zone and will travel as often as nightly, so it needs to be durable. For younger children, teachers often issue (or require) two-pocket folders, designating one side "Take Home" and the other "Bring Back." If your child has demonstrated success with this system in years past, it's best to stick with it. If pocket folders don't work, however, try file folders, top-loading "backpack" folders, or an accordion file divided either by subject or by whether the paper stays home or goes back-to-school. Whatever your child chooses, it should be big enough to hold a stack of papers, but not so big that a single sheet of paper gets swallowed up; and, as previously mentioned, it should be durable. Many teachers have a required system for this, so before your child gets too excited, make sure his or her system will be acceptable to the teacher.

A CONTAINER FOR SCHOOL SUPPLIES

Possible storage solutions for pencils, erasers, and all the other things that invariably end up in the desk will vary widely based on your child's age, taste, and styles, along with teacher requirements; some teachers specify not only the case, but what must go inside as well. Younger kids tend to gravitate to pencil boxes (and a pencil box may even be on the required supply list) or fancy pencil pouches. Size is a key factor here and will vary depending on what must be kept inside and where it will be stored in the classroom.

If no container is specified, let your child's styles be your guide. Those with an *I love stuff* personal style will likely go for fun or unique containers, while those with an *I need to see it* personal style or an *I know I put it somewhere* organizational style might opt for clear containers. Those with a *cram and jam* organizational style need something spacious enough to accommodate cramming and jamming, but small enough to fit wherever the teacher requires supplies to be stored. These kids, like those with a *drop and run* organizational style or an *I love to be busy* personal style, often benefit from open containers they can simply drop supplies into. In the absence of these containers, kids with these styles might just stash everything in their desks — a big, rectangular space — where small objects tend to disappear into the abyss.

Older kids who travel between classrooms often like flat pencil cases designed to fit inside three-ring binders. These kids are typically carrying fewer supplies at one time than their younger peers, and portability is more important than capacity. In schools where students are allowed to carry backpacks from class to class, the backpack itself may suffice. If the backpack must stay in the locker during the school day, it (along with the locker itself) can serve as a storage area for writing implements, extra paper, and other supplies.

ONE MORE THING ...

If your child's school doesn't supply a planner, you and your child might want to talk about his or her plan for keeping track of assignments. Kids in the primary grades don't typically need a planner, but by middle school a planner might be something you want to add to your shopping list. In elementary school, as long as kids are in the same classroom all day long, they're less likely to lose track of assignments. But once they start having language arts in one classroom and math, science, and/or social studies in another, it's time to develop a system for keeping track of what's due when.

Most kids don't need anything fancy — just something with enough space to write their assignments. Initially, a simple assignment notebook might do the trick, but as long-term projects enter the picture, it's time to introduce a calendar as part of the setup. Whatever you and your child choose, be sure to give the assignment notebook or planner a good home. After all, if your child can't find it, he can't use it. Your child may choose to integrate it into his or her **home for papers to deal with**, or carry it separately, depending on the tool he or she decides to use for the papers that travel between home and school. Even when schools provide online access to assignments, many kids remember the details better if they physically write the assignment down.

LIVING IN THE REAL WORLD

At school, your child might not have a choice of systems or containers. Many teachers believe that there is one way to organize, and that is the plan they model for their students. For many students this leads to success, further entrenching the one-size-fits-all philosophy.

I was so grateful to the fifth-grade teachers who allowed me to bring Organizing by STYLE into their classrooms; they were willing to let their students experiment with different organizers and different plans. But if the students weren't actually using the systems they selected, or those systems weren't working as expected, it was time to either go the traditional route or come up with a Plan B that worked. I thought that was a fair deal all around.

If you're the parent of a child who organizes differently, you might need to intervene on your child's behalf, especially if your child has been in school long enough for it to have become clear that the traditional route does not work. Still, suggesting that your child be an exception to the required materials rule may or may not go over well. Together with your child, decide if it's better to work within the requirements (buy the required binder, but adapt its insides so your child can use it successfully) or seek the teacher's stamp of approval for an alternate system. If your child's teacher understands that the required tool is actually a stumbling block, he or she may be amenable to a trial period with something else. Most teachers are happy to see their students attempt organization, no matter which tools they use; in the best-case scenario, your child's teacher might become an ally who helps to tweak and perfect the plan.

WHAT DO I DO WITH ALL THIS STUFF AT HOME?

Just as students need a few basics for keeping their school stuff in order, so do parents, who get inundated with forms to sign, papers to read, and information to file. And then there are the supplies — backpacks full of school stuff as well as various and sundry bags laden with sports equipment, musical instruments, and other extracurricular supplies.

As more and more schools go paperless, some of these storage concerns diminish, but electronic storage is not the plan of choice for some of the styles. At our house, although the cafeteria menu was available online 24/7, I printed out a copy and tacked it to the bulletin board in the kitchen. Because my personal style is *I need to see it*, having the menu visible facilitated planning and actually saved time, because once it was printed I didn't need to keep looking it up online. I also hung on to the halves of permission slips that detailed field-trip information (some parents prefer to write the details on the calendar, then throw the paper away). In addition, I kept a file of policy-related papers. For me, "paperless" on the school end meant I was the one doing the printing, because I operate better with a tangible hard copy than an amorphous online version.

Once you decide what you actually need to store in terms of school paperwork, how you set up the storage is between you and your styles. Any container that works for you — a binder, an accordion folder, a clipboard, a file drawer, a dedicated file container, or something else entirely — is a workable solution. Not sure? Ask yourself which storage system will require minimal time to create *and* will let you easily put your hands on the information you need as your child is running out the door asking you the question only those papers can answer.

Keeping track of paper flow is also a consideration. Creating a drop spot for the papers your kids bring home — papers for you to read and/or sign and/or return to school — will minimize lost papers and last-minute headaches. Decide where you want this drop spot and let your kids know that's where any actionable papers go. The designated drop spot doesn't need to be fancy, or even a container. It simply needs to be a logical match for your styles (*I need to see it* parents shouldn't choose a drawer, for example) and accessible to your kids. Don't forget to make it clear to your kids where you'll put the papers after you finish with them. Will your kids need to reclaim them from the same spot? Will you hand them directly back to the child in question? Who makes sure they get into the backpack? Your styles and your child's styles, age, and level of accountability should guide your plan.

This same philosophy works for storing the big stuff as well. Will bags and backpacks have a drop spot in a shared family space, or do all those belongings go into the rooms of their owners? If those belongings live in shared space, where do they go so they're out of the way? Whose responsibility will it be to take action on those items when they need to go to school (the instrument on band day), be washed, repaired, or refilled (sports uniforms, lunch boxes, other supplies)?

Last, but perhaps most important, is keeping track of dates, times, appointments, and so on. Having a system for keeping track of these obligations will reduce the likelihood of running into a situation where everyone has to be in a different place at the same time. As with all the other systems, this one can take whatever form works for the keeper of the calendar. It should be accessible (and perhaps even visible) to everyone; guidelines for who adds to it and who keeps track of it will vary based on your family's styles and your children's ages. Some families like color-coded calendars, while others prefer binders or dry-erase boards; as long as it works, the form it takes is up to you.

The systems you model, set up, and help your kids set up for their school things provide real-world, hands-on lessons in organization for the long haul. Keep in mind that your goal isn't simply a solution for the school year, but rather long-term organizational skills. This perspective can help reduce frustration as you work with your kids to create systems that work for them.

KNOW THYSELF

When my daughter was growing up, my husband and I often argued over the same thing: expecting her to pick up after herself. If she'd leave a dish on the table or her shoes in the middle of the floor or some other belonging somewhere it didn't belong, he'd tell her to pick it up. She'd take her sweet time, waiting him out.

Guess who usually won.

Tired of looking at the dish, tripping over the shoes, or arguing over the belonging, my husband would take care of it because it bothered him.

I, on the other hand, have been known to leave my daughter's cereal bowl from breakfast — with milk still in it — on the dining room table until she came home from school. If the rule was "put your dishes in the sink," I had no intention of doing it for her.

I love my daughter, and I'm happy to do things for her, and I don't take a hard line on many rules. But not expecting her to do things for herself isn't doing her any favors. No one (except her father) will pick up after her, so she needs to learn to do it herself. It's not only a basic building block of organization, but a life skill as well.

My daughter is now a young adult. Her tolerance for disorder is lower than mine and higher than my husband's. Her room can get only so messy before she decides — on her own — that she needs to do something about it. Once an *I love stuff* kid, she is now more ruthless about getting rid of things she no longer needs, in part because the same mom who left a cereal bowl on the table all day allowed her the freedom to decide when it was time to part with things that I deemed trash but that she classified as treasure.

But I can't take all the credit. My daughter's unique organizational preferences and methods were shaped merely by the examples my husband and I set and the parenting we provided. Our daughter is an individual in her own right, created by God not to be a carbon copy of me or her father, but as someone with her own talents and treasures. By providing examples of what to do (and what not to do) and by setting basic rules and expectations, we can point her in the right direction, but in the end, the path is one she needs to pave. Giving her the opportunity to experiment within the structure of our home honored her uniqueness while providing parameters she could accept or reject when it came time to put her own house in order.

Each household is different. How can you find a comfortable intersection between your children's styles and your own?

Smart organizers know when to ask for help.
Dear Lord, help me to support my children and be their advocate, even when their styles differ from my own. Help me always to be a confidence builder and to let my children know that they are more important to me than tidiness and conformity. Amen.

LISA'S LISTS
Adapt-an-Organizer

Small adaptations can make a big difference.

Which of the following might help your child take a baby step toward organization at school?

1. Inside that required three-ring binder for the nonbinder person:

   - a portable three-hole punch
   - page protectors (just slide those unpunched pages in)
   - folder pockets
   - binder clips at the front and back for times when they're in a hurry and/or the holes aren't already punched in the papers (they can even be color-coded to match the binder)
   - an acetate envelope with a string or Velcro closure (look for one with binder holes)

2. Instead of a three-ring binder:

   - an accordion folder (one for each subject in middle or high school)
   - a binder with spring-loaded clamp (no rings, so no holes necessary — plus it's fun to play with)
   - a set of bound pocket folders
   - an acetate envelope with a string or Velcro closure for each subject (which can be color-coded by subject)

3. Instead of traditional paper pocket folders:

    - file folders (which can be color-coded by class)
    - an acetate folder or envelope (one per class)
    - transparent folders, with or without pockets
    - top-loading "backpack" folders

CHAPTER 11

Time Management

*For everything there is a season, and a
time for every matter under heaven.*
ECCLESIASTES 3:1

For most of this book, we've been talking about tools to keep our stuff organized, but I'd be remiss if I didn't spend a little time talking about how to keep our lives organized. When it comes to that monumental task, two tools spring to mind: lists and planners. These two tools are among my favorites because they can so easily be personalized to meet our individual needs. In addition, they're easy to play with and change up without making a mess or going to great expense.

Surprised? Let's take a look.

LISTS

Just as our styles guide our choices of the tools we use for keeping our stuff organized, they also guide our choices when it comes to list-making and planners. Believe it or not, there's more than one way to make a list. See if you can identify each of the personal and organizational styles in the list-making approaches below:

- I have a lovely planner with room for lists, but I end up using slips of paper instead because once I close the planner the list "disappears."
- I make lists for everything and then put them in a place that makes sense at the time. Later, when I need them, I can't remember where I put them.
- I cram everything onto one, big, long list. Heaven help me if I ever lose it.
- I jot down what I need as I go, writing tasks on whatever paper happens to be handy.
- Lists? Of course I have lists! But sometimes just looking at them makes me tired.
- Lists? I'm all set! I have an entire collection of notepads and matching pens. If only they weren't too pretty to use …

Just as with organizing, matching your list-making method to how you think can help things run more smoothly. Whether you're the *I need to see it* list maker whose list has to be an open book, the *cram and jammer* with a master list that goes on for days, a *drop and run* or *I know I put it somewhere* organizer with multiple lists, an *I love to be busy person* with a totally overwhelming list or an *I love stuff* collector with so many notepads and so few actual lists, both you and your lists will be more efficient if you adjust your method to match your style.

Let's take another look at the list conundrums and tweak them a bit to make them more efficient.

THE PERSONAL STYLES

The *I need to see it* situation: I have a lovely planner with room for lists, but I end up using slips of paper instead because once I close the planner, the list disappears.

The upgrade: First, decide whether you want to keep your lists inside or outside — of your planner, that is. Outside? Try clipping a sheet of paper to the front of your planner. That way, your list(s) and your planner are together, but your list is visible. If you're brave enough to close the book on your lists, try tabbing the list pages inside the planner with sticky flags so you can flip right to them. You can even create multiple lists and color-code them. Can't decide between inside and out? If your planner is big enough, tuck a small clipboard with a few sheets of paper into your planner and make your lists there. (Notepads are nice but can make the planner unwieldy.) Not feeling the need to pair your lists and your planner? Don't worry about it. If your outside-the-planner system is working, don't change it!

The *I love to be busy* situation: Lists? Of course I have lists! But sometimes just looking at them makes me tired.

The upgrade: Combine your planner and your lists. Whether you buy a planner with space for list-making or attach a sticky note to each calendar page so your to-dos line up with your where-to-be-whens, having the opportunity to jot things down in the moment can save time and help keep things running smoothly. You might not have any less to do, but you'll need to look in only one place to find the what, the where, and the when.

The *I love stuff* situation: Lists? I'm all set! I have an entire collection of notepads and matching pens. If only they weren't too pretty to use ...

The upgrade: Buy duplicates — one notepad to use, one to appreciate. After all, shouldn't your notes be pretty if you want them to be? Or get a pretty box where you can keep a collection of the first page of every notepad. Then use the rest of the notepad for its intended purpose.

THE ORGANIZATIONAL STYLES

The *I know I put it somewhere* situation: I make lists for everything and then put them in a place that makes sense at the time. Later, when I need them, I can't remember where I put them.

The upgrade: Establish locations for your lists and make sure they stick — literally. A magnetic notepad on the fridge. A whiteboard or write-on/wipe-off calendar. A notepad stuck to a bulletin board. A sticky notepad in a bedside drawer. Corral all those notepads and assign them a limited number of homes; then develop the habit of using only those notepads ... or be sure to stick free-floating notes scribbled in a hurry to one of those spots. Immediately.

The *cram and jam* situation: I cram everything onto one big, long list. Heaven help me if I ever lose it.

The upgrade: As long as you can keep track of the list and read everything on it, there's no problem to be solved here. Make sure you know when to switch to a clean piece of paper because the old one is too full or hard to read. In addition, consider making a copy of the list or taking a picture of it with your phone so you have a backup if it ever goes missing. Otherwise, if the length of the list doesn't stress you out, keep up the good work!

The *drop and run* situation: I jot down what I need as I go, writing tasks on whatever paper happens to be handy.

The upgrade: Not a problem — just collect your wayward lists and combine them onto one list or find a way to corral the slips of paper. You can staple them together, collect them on a small clipboard, keep them together with a binder clip or a paper clip, or use a magnet to stick them to the fridge, white board, or file cabinet. Or you can make sticky notes your go-to for list making, and then all your notes will stick together without a problem. Writing something down when you think of it is a great strategy. As long as you can keep track of your collection, having a stash of notes isn't a bad thing.

Have you noticed that these methods were (mostly) on the right track all along? In no case did I say, "Stop doing that!" When we list by style, it's effortless, even if the tasks themselves are not. Making a big to-do out of to-do lists is a waste of time and defeats the purpose of this essential time-management strategy.

THERE'S MORE THAN ONE WAY TO MAKE A LIST

List making can be a straightforward proposition, or we can get creative. Even a basic list scrawled on scrap paper can be subdivided, color-coded, categorized, or some combination of the above. These additional steps can help us identify the most necessary or time-sensitive tasks with a single glance.

In his book *The Seven Habits of Highly Effective People*, Stephen Covey introduced quadrants based on urgency and importance for managing time and tasks. This list-making method lets us see at a glance what matters most (and what's most urgent) rather than falsely assume that every item on the list is equally important — which is rarely the case. By spending most of our time on the things that are important, but not urgent, we can keep on top of our lives and avoid getting stressed out.

Urgent and important	Not urgent but important
Urgent but not important	Neither urgent nor important

Another way to subdivide lists is to group items by task, such as things to do, things to buy, and contacts to make; alternatively, we can choose to subdivide by category (work tasks, home tasks, recreation/family tasks). Although you can purchase notepads with headings like these, you can just as easily make your own simply by subdividing a blank page.

If you want to make your lists a bit fancier or more visual, you can color-code them, using highlighters or different-colored pens to subdivide by category, day, or any other grouping that works for you. This strategy is often second nature to those with an *I need to see it* personal style and helps them to keep their lists organized. In fact, when it comes to lists with style, *I love stuff* or *I need to see it* people might be onto something with pretty paper, fancy pens, and color-coded or highlighted to-do lists that draw our attention to specific items. Bullet journals, the ultimate in pretty to-do lists, often include elements of sketch-noting such as artistic lettering, fancy borders, and important tasks subdivided into boxes of their own.

Perhaps you're looking for something a bit simpler. Maybe long lists stress you out, or you prefer your lists more functional than fashionable. Choosing a set number of items to focus on each day and writing them into a planner can help us to stay focused. Outside of the school year, I often jot down three things I want to accomplish each day. You might choose two or five, depending on the size of the tasks and the time you have available. The important thing is to make the short list realistic. Planning to clean the house from top to bottom, redecorate the living room, and organize the garage is clearly unrealistic, but choosing one step that takes you closer to each of these goals can move you in the right direction.

Whether we specifically integrate our lists with our planners or not, at some point these two tools need to meet. Regardless of where we choose to make our lists, if we get into the habit of assigning a time and date to each task, we're more likely to finish our to-dos, leading us to the lovely satisfaction of crossing completed items off the list. Crossing things off the list is, in my opinion, one of the best reasons to make a list in the first place.

Finally, on those days when it feels as though we're spinning our wheels, moving busily from task to task but not managing to get to anything that's actually on the list, a backward to-do list might be in order. Creating such a list is simple. Instead of creating a list of things to do at the beginning of the day, take some time at the end of the day to create a "did-it" list, jotting down all the things you accomplished.

You might just be surprised at how productive you really were.

PLANNERS

The second key tool in time management is a planner — the one I've been referring to frequently in this chapter. Not surprisingly, our styles impact our choice of planners. I love my electronics and rarely go anywhere without my cell phone, but when it comes to planners, my *I need to see it* style prevails —

I'm a paper-and-pencil girl. I'm also very specific about what my planner needs to have and, I admit, I've spent way too much money more than once on the "perfect" planner. I look for planners that have room to write and have even upsized a little when the slightly bigger planner had better features than the one that tucked easily into my purse.

Think about the purpose(s) you want your planner to serve. Will it travel with you from place to place so you can note appointments on the run? Will you use the same planner for work and home? Do you want a planner that functions as a daily diary, with space for lists and notes as well as appointments? Will you forgo the planner entirely for something wall-mounted that includes the important dates for everyone in the family? Finally, will one master planner do the trick?

While having a single planner that holds everything is a good idea in theory, it doesn't work for everyone — and I'm one of the people it *doesn't* work for. Because I use my work planner as more than a calendar, my home, family, and writing obligations tend to get lost amid the planning and deadlines. Consequently, I have one planner for work, one for writing projects, and one for everything else. I'm sure this would make any professional organizer worth her salt cringe in horror, but it works for me.

The purpose of your planner will determine its *size* (small and portable? large and comprehensive? desk-sized?), *view* (day by day? month by month? week at a glance?), and *features* (contacts? space for notes? reference pages?). Beyond that, it comes down to price and aesthetics and, of course, your styles.

Not sure what you want? Try doing some window-shopping in the planner aisle of an office supply store. Or, if you're doing this in December or January, you might even be able to pick up a few of the complimentary calendars many businesses offer for the upcoming year. One of those freebies might just be the perfect fit. If not, by the time you've finished playing and have refined your planner must-have list, your perfect planner might even be on sale.

Although time management is a challenge, knowing and embracing our styles helps us choose the tools that work for us so we can take charge of our time instead of feeling as though it's slipping through our fingers.

KNOW THYSELF

I spend an inordinate amount of time trying to find the sweet spot between procrastination and productivity. If such a spot exists, it's elusive, to say the least.

Most of the time, I seem to lean toward one extreme or the other. On productive days, I feel as though I've conquered time management, and when I string a few of these days together, I feel very virtuous as I check one thing after another off my list.

And then the pendulum swings. All the energy I reveled in disappears and I wrap myself in a woolen blanket of procrastination. Some days the blanket is more warm than itchy, and I'm loath to relinquish it and face the things I should be doing. Other days it's just itchy enough to spur me into action.

After a little time spent beneath it, of course.

Rest is important. Even the Lord God rested, and he asks us to dedicate an entire day each week to rest and renewal; yet, in our quest for productivity, we often forget this.

Some weeks, balance will be elusive. Other weeks, it will be impossible. But when we find time to curl up under that blanket, whether because we're hiding from our responsibilities temporarily or because we're wisely renewing ourselves, it's important to conserve energy, not waste it beating ourselves up.

The Lord had a busy six days creating the heavens and the earth. And then he rested. He didn't make excuses or feel guilty about it. He is wise enough to teach us that rest is a necessity, not a luxury.

We're called to do many things and be many things, but as we plan our weeks, we'd be wise to remember to pencil in time for rest, renewal, and prayer. Without them, everything else is so much harder than it has to be.

Smart organizers know when to ask for help.
Dear Lord, help me to be a good steward of the time you have given me and to use each day wisely, well, and according to your will. Amen.

LISA'S LISTS

Seven Ways to Zoom in on the Planner That's Right for You

So many planners, so little time.

Here are a few questions to ask as you enter into a partnership with this time management tool.

1. **In style or my style?** Just because it works for someone else doesn't mean it will work for you. If you're looking for a long-term planner relationship, choose one that suits your styles.

2. **To tech or not to tech?** Just because you carry a phone doesn't mean your calendar has to be on it. Depending on your styles, old-fashioned just might beat newfangled.

3. **Fashionable, functional, or both?** As with books, you can't judge a planner by its cover, but if the pretty cover will make you more likely to use it, that's an incentive worth considering.

4. **Parked or portable?** Whether your calendar is staying at home or traveling with you, be sure to give it a consistent home. If you can't find it, you can't use it.

5. **Long term or short term?** Think about how far ahead you plan and how much space you need for keeping track of your obligations. If most of your planning occurs on a day-by-day or week-by-week basis, you might be just as happy with a

wall calendar and a notepad divided by days of the week.

6. **Permanent or semi-permanent?** I rarely write anything in my planner in ink unless it's a special date like a birthday or anniversary. My daughter (and many of my college students) swears by whiteboards that allow them to edit deadlines and tasks as they come and go.

7. **One of a kind or a matched set?** Contrary to conventional organizational wisdom, the single-master-planner rule can be broken as long as you have a system for tying all the to-do threads together.

CHAPTER 12

Pep Talks and
Parting Thoughts

For nothing will be impossible with God.
LUKE 1:37

Congratulations! You've done it! You've made it to the end of the book!

I must admit, however, that I've become rather attached to talking to you about Organizing by STYLE and I'm not quite ready to end our chat, so I'd like to do one more thing before I close.

As you know by now, organization is a process. Because this is the case, we can sometimes feel as though we'll never arrive at our organization destination. When you find yourself overwhelmed, unsure, or in need of a refresher, open the book to this chapter. Here you'll find simple reminders, which I hope will function as a five-minute troubleshooting session/pep talk so you don't have to feel alone or unprepared as you face the next step in the organization process.

Consider it one last Lisa's List.

See that? And you thought you were rid of me.

You've got this. Go forth bravely, Organizing by STYLE.

I CAN'T GET STARTED!

Where you get started matters less than getting started in the first place.

Start in the space that's least overwhelming. Is there a spot you can reclaim quickly? Small successes motivate us to move on to bigger organizational challenges. Eliminating one pile can actually make us *feel* lighter and maybe more inclined to tackle another hot spot.

Start in the space that matters most. Beginning with the place you most want to reclaim gives you built-in motivation and builds confidence.

Start in the space that bugs you the most. Is there a place in your home that's become a dumping ground — one you're not quite sure how to fix? Set a timer and chip away at it until time's up. Shrinking the pile will give you a sense of accomplishment and a clearer idea of what you need to do next.

Start at the bottom. I wish I could take credit for this idea, but the truth is I heard it long ago on HGTV and have been using it ever since. With clothing and paper in particular, the oldest or least frequently used items are usually on the bottom of the pile or in the back of the closet. Outdated and forgotten, they're relatively easy to get rid of. This can give us the boost we need to keep digging until the pile is gone.

I CAN'T LET IT GO!

Try asking yourself a few questions to clarify what's worth keeping and what isn't.

Is it hazardous, dangerous, or otherwise a threat to physical or emotional safety? If so, let it go. If not, move along to the next question.

Does it take up more than its fair share of space? If it's easy enough to tuck the item in question away, go ahead and keep it if it matters to you. If you need to make space for it, are tripping over it, and it doesn't hold meaning for anyone else, consider letting it go.

Will someone else love this? Quite honestly, the answer to this question is usually no; but for some items, like clothing, books, and toys in good condition, consigning, donating, or otherwise passing them along can make it easier to say goodbye. Be sure you have a definite destination in mind, though, as well as a plan for getting it there. Otherwise it's all too easy to simply move a thing from one spot to another instead of moving it out.

Does it fit? I'm not talking just about clothing here. A piece of furniture that's too big for the space, a container that's too small to hold everything it needs to, an organizer that doesn't match your styles … all these are candidates for the trash, recycling bin, or another home.

Does it serve a purpose? Enhancing the beauty of your living space is a valid purpose, but we can only keep so many things because they're pretty. The best items — especially containers and organizers — are those that are both pretty and practical.

CLEAR SPACE DOESN'T STAY CLEAR!

Hot spots often don't extinguish easily.

Stake your claim. While our eventual goal may be a lot of clear space, this is no small feat in a busy household. Choose one clear space that matters to you and declare it a "no clutter/ no dumping" zone. Go public, letting your family know that this space is off-limits to *all* clutter. Items that have homes should go where they belong, and homeless items need to land somewhere else.

Practice what you preach. That "no clutter" rule goes for the declutterer too. If this is newly claimed space and breaking the dumping habit proves challenging, put the "Don't put it down, put it away!" guideline into action. This simple change can grow into a habit that allows you to preserve that coveted clear space.

Is it always the same counter? Most homes have spots that are clutter catchers — the kitchen counter, the dining room table, the dresser in the bedroom. Ask yourself whether the items that are piled there should be stored nearby, or if the spot is merely convenient. Then organize accordingly.

Is it always the same stuff? At my house, it's usually the homeless items that end up in piles in predictable locations — right alongside the piles of things that serve as my visual list. While I can't quite bring myself to get rid of the reminder piles, eliminating the piles of homeless items is as simple as finding them a home.

Will a strategically placed container solve the problem? If piles in this hot spot are inevitable, maybe, just maybe corralling them and keeping them under wraps is a viable solution. Just make sure that the container you choose is the right size for the job. Too big, and it will eat up the clear space all by itself. Too small, and you'll end up with overflow that mimics the problem you were trying to eliminate.

IT'S ALL TOO MUCH!

Aim for progress, not perfection.

Identify the obstacle. Often, when these feelings emerge, something has gotten in the way of our progress. Maybe it's a shortage of time, maybe it's an influx of stuff, maybe it's that one spot that just won't stay organized. Temporary setbacks are not the same as permanent problems. Keep using your style-specific strategies, and this too shall pass.

Work in short bursts. Better to **Give it five!** and see progress than let things sit (or get worse) until you have the perfect time block in which to organize them perfectly. Set a timer, and when time's up — whether it's five minutes or an hour — pat yourself on the back for perfectly completing your time block instead of beating yourself up for not making the space look perfect.

Take strategic breaks. No matter how long the list, you can't work 24/7. You'll be much more efficient if you remember to give your body and brain a break. It can feel counterintuitive to stop working when there's still a lot to do, but the goal is to keep the momentum going and forestall exhaustion. When you feel yourself stalling, growing increasingly indecisive, or getting cranky, you need a break.

Remember, it's a process. Identifying your personal and organizational styles is the first step in this one-step-forward-two-steps-back process. Some days you'll feel like an organizational guru, and other days you'll feel like the Queen or King of Chaos. Keep taking those baby steps and don't forget to focus on your successes.

IT'S NOT WORKING,
BUT I'M NOT SURE WHY

Even the best systems need tweaking sometimes.

Is this a temporary problem? Certain times of the year and certain seasons of life are naturally more hectic. If you're in one of those seasons and the problem will resolve itself in reasonably short order, consider using short-term solutions instead of revamping your entire system.

Does everything here belong here? Consider whether or not extraneous and/or homeless items are part of the problem. If so, remove them, then reassess.

Have things with out-of-the-way homes crept into a more convenient location? While it makes sense to store things we use only occasionally in out-of-the-way locations (especially when space is an issue), the things we use more often need to be easier to access. Remember the rules of location: store items as close as possible to where they're used, store frequently used items in easy-to-access places, store similar items together, and consider whether or not a new home for some things will solve the problem.

Is the system easy to use? When putting things away is difficult, we choose the path of least resistance, putting things down instead of away (*drop and run* organizers), putting them wherever there's space (*I know I put it somewhere* organizers), or stuffing them somewhere (*cram and jammers*). When we do this, we exacerbate the problem, creating a retrieval issue. If this is what's happening, look for ways to simplify your system.

Are my systems overwhelmed? Did I choose "just right" containers instead of tools that allow me (and my possessions) room to grow? Are there things here that don't belong here? Once everything is where it belongs, reassess your containers and systems to see if an upgrade is needed.

Do my systems fit both my styles and my lifestyle? If they fit my personal and organizational styles but require a more time-consuming process than my schedule permits, it might be time to revamp. There's no shame in simplifying a system, especially if that makes it more efficient.

Do I like it? Although how much we like a tool or system might not affect how well it works, our feelings can affect how likely we are to use it. If it's functional (a worn accordion file with just the right number of labeled sections, for example), we might not care how it looks, especially if we tuck it away in a drawer or closet. But, if you're taking your system from so-so to spectacular, the aesthetics of containers and systems are worth considering.

When all else fails, throw some STYLE at it: *celebrate successes, take small steps, find logical and consistent homes,* and *let go* of the stuff you don't love. Before you know it, the *upkeep* will be *easy* — or at least easier — and even better, you'll have the confidence you need to keep the process going.

Smart organizers know when to ask for help.
Dear Lord, help me to remember that getting organized isn't just something I can check off my list. When I feel overwhelmed by this ongoing process, help me to lean on you and to use the gifts you have given me so I can continue to make progress. Amen.

Acknowledgments

This book was more than a decade in the making, and I'm grateful to everyone who helped me take these concepts from ideas to classroom lessons to my blog to this page.

Thanks ...

... always to my mom, who taught me there's a place for everything (and everything in its place), and to my dad who, as a Realtor, taught me the importance of location, location, location. Without their love and support, this whole writing gig would never have happened.

... to my East York Elementary School family, especially Jill Amspacher, who entrusted me with her third-graders for my first-ever organizing small group, and the fourth- and fifth-grade teachers who welcomed me and my crazy ideas about organization into their classrooms more than a decade ago: Jess Barley, Stef Crumbling, Lisa Eckenrode, Brandon Gerber, Stacy Houck, Cheryl Johnson, Missy Miller, Katie Pringle, Pat Rinkevich, Wendy Ross, Amy Valdez, Donna Biser, Dwight Hare, and Jaime Wolf — as well as Scott Weaver, who sent me some of his kids who were gifted and talented in subject matter, but not always in organization. And, of course, to my students who were my partners in trying on and refining the styles with the crazy names.

... to Sarah Reinhard, who inspired me to keep blogging and who brought me first into the CatholicMom.com family, and then into the Our Sunday Visitor family, both of which are pretty cool families to be a part of. Thanks also to Mary Beth Baker and Rebecca Willen at Our Sunday Visitor, who sharpened my ideas and my prose and brought this book to life.

... to the amazing Barb Szyszkiewicz, who asked if I might want to write a back-to-school column for CatholicMom.com (which turned into STYLE Savvy) and who has been my cheerleader every step of the way. Thanks also to Lisa Hendey (and then Danielle Bean) who agreed to let me take up that space week after week and find my audience.

190 | Acknowledgments

... to the fellow writers I count among my friends: my sister Lori Cramer; my writing accountability partner and friend, Cerella Sechrist; friend and reader of late-night emails, Laurie Edwards; and Pennwriters pals Johanna Greenlaw and Angel Prichard. Thanks also to my critique group, especially Anne Kline, Mike Wertz, Jackie Werth, and Judy Wolfman who read this book in its very early stages, giving me feedback and ideas. Special thanks to Anne Kline who read it again before I hit "send" on the manuscript and would accept only a cup of coffee as thanks.

And always, for Steve and Leah, who put up with all my writing stories and insecurities, and who are on the receiving end of my glares when I'm writing and they dare to want to ask me a question. I love you both for your patience, but mostly just because of who you are.

About the Author

Lisa Lawmaster Hess is a transplanted Jersey girl who has lived in Pennsylvania for most of her adult life. She is the author of two nonfiction books (*Acting Assertively* and *Diverse Divorce*) and two novels (*Casting the First Stone* and *Chasing a Second Chance*). In addition, she has written columns for local publications and articles for national and online publications, including *Pediatrics for Parents, Faculty Focus, Teachers of Vision*, and *Today's Catholic Teacher*.

Lisa is also a contributor to *50 Over 50: A Collection of Established and Emerging Women Writers, The Catholic Mom's Prayer Companion*, and *Stage Directions Guide to Getting and Keeping Your Audience*. Lisa blogs at The Porch Swing Chronicles and Organizing by STYLE, and is a contributor at CatholicMom. com. A retired elementary school counselor, Lisa is an adjunct professor of psychology at York College of Pennsylvania.

Want more? Check out Lisa's blog,
Organizing by STYLE, at orgbystyle.blogspot.com.